SEEKING THE HOLY

An Introduction to the History and Practice of Spiritual Direction for Today's Churches

ISRAEL GALINDO

Seeking the Holy:
An Introduction to the History and Practice of Spiritual Direction
for Today's Churches
Israel Galindo
Copyright © 2015, Israel Galindo
All rights reserved.

No part of this publication may be reproduced, stored in a retrieval system, or transmitted in any form or by any other means, electronic, mechanical, photocopying, recording, or otherwise, without the prior permission of the copyright owner, except for brief quotations included in a review of the book.

Chapter 2 appeared previously as "Spiritual Direction and Pastoral Care," in *Spiritual Direction and the Care of Souls,* Moon and Benner, eds. (Intervarsity Press 2004).

Cover: "Seeking the Holy" by Israel Galindo

Published by Educational Consultants

Contents

Introduction 4

1. Historical Perspectives 10

2. Spiritual Direction, Counseling, and Therapy 26

3. The Goals of Spiritual Direction 41

4. The Process of Spiritual Direction 48

5. Spiritual Direction and the Congregational Context 62

Bibliography

Notes

Introduction

I grew up in a Christian home, with devout parents who lived and practiced their faith. They were faithful church members who saw to the religious formation of their children. In later years my father became a minister and as a result, being intimately involved in the life of a church community became part of the formative experience for my siblings and me.

Church attendance was not a passive spectator sport growing up. As with most who grow up in small churches, there were plenty of opportunities for participation in all aspects of church life. Small churches often do a better job of providing formative experiences through the corporate practices of a faith community. We learned to pray by praying alongside adults and church leaders. We were welcomed to eavesdrop on sincere, often heated, theological conversations among the adults. We were given leadership responsibilities early, from assisting and teaching Sunday School to church committee responsibilities. Through both teachings and supportive relationships we learned that God was a loving presence in our lives on whom we could depend and find meaning in the midst of any circumstance.

Seeking the Holy

Growing up in that environment was powerfully formative. In mind, spirit, and practice, I was Christian. Faith was a defining part of my psyche. You can imagine how surprising it was, then, to reach a point in life in my 30s, when the faith of my formation became inadequate for the later stage in life.

Despite my seminary training, Bible study became stale and almost meaningless. Critical-exegetical habits of reading scripture were useful for sermon preparation, but no longer fed mind or heart. I needed to learn to read the Bible a different way, but did not know how. Despite years in the practice of prayer, it now became unsatisfactory and almost empty. There was, as far as I knew, only one way to pray, and it was no longer working. Participation in church became routine and un-motivating. Even the relationships with church friends became frustrating as I began to ask questions that seemed not to connect with them. New questions of meaning were met with familiar quick answers that now seemed trite, and often, intellectually dishonest.

By way of being a "crisis of faith," my experience was a relatively mild one. In terms of a "dark night of the soul," it did not move much beyond an uncertain dusk, a losing sight of the guiding stars that had helped navigate the journey of faith. Nevertheless, my restlessness was enough to cause me to seek answers to questions I had not previously asked. However, the streams that had formerly quenched the yearnings of the soul were no longer adequate. The streams still flowed, and I observed that while others received nourishment from them, for me, they were neither refreshing nor fulfilling.

During those years I entered into spiritual direction. I had read enough about the practice to believe that was what I needed to address the spiritual malaise I was experiencing. I found a wonderful spiritual guide in a Cenacle retreat house. Sister Barbara became my spiritual director. Under her guidance some amazing things happened: I learned to pray for the first time in my life; I discovered new dimensions in my relationship with God, I found resolution (though not always answers) to the deeper questions of faith—some of which I had not been able to formulate yet. Discipleship, growth in faith, spiritual disciplines like reading the Bible and prayer, all took on newness, but more importantly, became meaningful once again.

Mine is not a unique story. Hundreds of contemporary Christians move through a similar trajectory in their spiritual journeys. Formed in the womb of Christian homes, reared in the formal educational programs and informal formational experiences of congregational church life, they take up the received faith of parents, a faith community, perhaps even of mentors. Most are content to stay there. Some, however, encounter a crisis of faith of some kind which uncovers the inadequacy of their current faith structure or belief system. Spiritual practices that were meaningful and sustaining no longer satisfy.

Others may outgrow the things most congregations are able to provide for a faith that yearns for something deeper. Still others are of the character that seeks continued personal growth. Some of these become seekers. They seek the Holy, a deeper relationship with God, a different way of believing. Some seek new ways of practicing faith, ready to commit to two paths, the inward journey and the outward journeys of faith. For many, the answer lies in the commitment to a relationship in spiritual direction.

Traditionally, spiritual direction has been considered a form of pastoral care in which matters of the spiritual life are given particular attention. Some definitions will be of help at this point. K. A. Wall defined the art simply as "The guiding of a Christian soul in the path of perfection." [1] Carroll and Dyckman offered this definition of spiritual direction: " . . . as interpersonal relationship in which one person assists others to reflect on their own experience in the light of who they are called to become in fidelity to the Gospel."[2] William A. Barry defined it as ". . . that form of pastoral counseling whose primary focus is to help another person (or persons) to develop a more conscious personal relationship with the mystery we call God."[3]

Sandra Schneiders added other elements to the practice of spiritual direction, describing it as ". . . a process carried out in the context of a one-to-one relationship in which a competent guide helps a fellow Christian to grow in the spiritual life by means of personal encounters that have the directee's spiritual growth as their explicit object."[4] Another significant element is identified in William A. Barry and William J. Connolly's definition: "The *focus* of . . . spiritual direction is on experience, not ideas, and specifically on religious experience, i.e., any experience of the mysterious Other whom we call God."[5] Max Thurian allowed for psychological and spiritual elements in his definition: "Spiritual direction, or the cure of souls, is a seeking after the leading of the Holy Spirit in a given psychological and spiritual situation.[6]

Writers on the practice of spiritual direction are careful to point out that the term 'spiritual' is not meant in an exclusive sense. The use of the term 'spiritual' in spiritual direction includes all aspects of a person's life structure.[7] Raymond Studzinski attempted to allay any fears arising from a negative connotation of the term 'direction':

> The process of spiritual direction does not involve one person telling another how to live and act. Direction for living and acting out is not found in the advice of a director as is some prefabricated scheme, but is the fabric of the individual's life which is being brought into sharper focus through the facilitating efforts of the director.[8]

The practice of spiritual direction has found expression in contemporary Christianity and in Protestant circles only recently. The needs left unmet by ignoring this practice have resulted, in Fairchild's opinion, in many adults being drawn to Pentecostal and charismatic renewal groups that promise a clearer image of, and more experimental in, the Spirit.[9] John H. Westerhoff III implied that this situation is a shifting of responsibility on the part of church leadership, who are responsible ". . . to equip the church with persons who can aid others on their journey toward internal and external perfection, the Spirit's gift of holy living of the perfect love of God and neighbor.[10]

This book provides a general introduction to the art and practice of spiritual direction. First, we will review brief history of the practice and development of spiritual direction. Second, salient elements of the practice of spiritual direction are identified and treated. The focus of this survey of the history and practice of spiritual direction is on: 1) the personalities which have shaped spiritual direction throughout the ages; 2) the educational dimensions of spiritual direction that are particularly relevant to the contemporary adults. We will also compare and contrast the practice of spiritual direction to pastoral counseling and psychotherapy in order to highlight their distinctiveness.

CHAPTER 1

Historical Perspectives

While recently rediscovered, relatively speaking, the practice of spiritual direction is an ancient one. Historically, it is associated with monasticism and auricular confession. In Catholic theology of the past two centuries, the term had come to be understood in the context of counseling individuals within the framework of sacramental confession. [11] Though spiritual direction in some form or another has existed since time immemorial (even outside of Christian tradition) this historical survey is restricted to its practice since New Testament times and within Christian traditions.

Spiritual Direction in the New Testament

Many writers make the claim that spiritual direction practices can be found in the New Testament. For them, Jesus emerges as the ideal spiritual director, both in his person and in the methods he used. His spiritual direction centered on the theme of *metanoia*. In the words of Tilden Edwards, "This then is the basic context for Jesus' guidance: the paradoxical transcendence and intimacy of God, and the fruits of Law, discernment, and empowered compassion.[12] Jesus' method of spiritual direction is interpreted from his use of symbolic language in parables, the cultivation of an intimate circle for special guidance, solitude, the observance of ritual, one-on-one and group interviews, and a call for personal commitment to God (*metanoia*).

Some writers also deem St. Paul to be an adept spiritual director. His letters reveal the personal care and the characteristics of a superlative spiritual guide of individuals and groups. His methods included journal writing, private and group interviewing, letter writing, preaching and teaching, modeling, and discipling. His epistles reveal his careful attention to the care of individuals through admonitions and the mentoring of younger disciples.

Spiritual Direction in the Early Church

In early Eastern Christianity spiritual direction developed chiefly for the formation of monks, though its roots were much broader. The desert fathers were specifically sought out for spiritual guidance. By the fourth century, the term *pneumatikos pater* was established in patristic literature.[13]

Seeking the Holy

The desert father Gregory of Neocaesares considered Origen as a spiritual guide and soul friend. According to church historian E. Glenn Hinson, Origen laid the foundations for the monastic spirituality that dominated Christian pastoral guidance throughout the Middle Ages. Origen delineated the traditional stages of the mystical journey, purgation, illumination, and union.[14] In fact, from the time of Origen until the Reformation, monasticism shaped the character of spiritual direction in the Church. During the late third century, the desert fathers (e.g., Gregory the Great, Anthony) gave spiritual direction its character. During this period seekers of the Holy sought out spiritual directors, particularly, who demonstrated discernment of spirits, considered a critical characteristic in the director.[15]

In early Western Christianity, St. Ambrose [c. 340-397] restricted himself to the spiritual direction of the beginner, stressing the fundamental Christian virtues of virginity and a moral life. St. Jerome [340-420] was also considered a talented spiritual director, and like Ambrose, stressed virginity and moral perfection. The great theologian and religious educator, St. Augustine [354-430], offered spiritual direction for both clergy and lay people based on the monastic model.

> ... He is important in the history of spiritual direction because of his efforts to set up and sustain monastic communities. This was the milieu in which he lived his own personal life from the time of his conversion. ... His counseling therefore tended to concentrate on it, but he replied also to particular requests for help from

individuals in every station of life. These replies gained him his reputation as an authority in spiritual direction.[16]

During the fifth and sixth centuries spiritual direction was given mainly to novices entering the monastic life. It was during this period that the Rule of Benedict (c. 529) gave the practice of spiritual direction a stable form through an outlined program of spiritual formation for clergy and lay persons.[17] The Rule stressed the importance of the spiritual director for the monastery, and a Christian education formation which was centered on the relationship between director and directee.[18] Religious educators such as Jonas of Orleans provided spiritual direction for lay persons outside of the monastery. He even wrote a seminal work on lay spiritual formation titled, *De Institutione Laicall* (*On Lay Training*).[19]

Spiritual Direction in the Middle Ages

During the twelfth century, spiritual direction reached a new zenith. St. Anselm of Canterbury (d. 1109) provided direction for the formation of monks as well as for others in every walk of life. Insisting on unceasing effort and continuing progress in one's spiritual life, "He taught that the primary goal was not the negative one of union with God."[20] A further step away from monastic spiritual direction was taken by St. Catherine of Siena (1347-1380) whose emphasis in direction was fundamentally charismatic.[21]

By far, the acknowledged spiritual director *par excellence* in the twelfth century was Bernard of Clairvaux (1090-1153).

Bernard stressed: 1) the importance of love in the direction of others; 2) submission to the director as being the prime object of ecclesiastical direction; and 3) the importance of choosing an able and discerning director.[22] St. Bonaventure (1221-1274) of the Franciscan school practiced a spiritual direction totally oriented toward the mystical. He further stressed the need for spiritual direction for most individuals in the initial stages of their spiritual formation.[23]

During the final centuries of the Middle Ages, the Dominican order focused its attention to giving spiritual direction to lay persons. This grew naturally from their mission of teaching and preaching. "The *cura animarum* thus became primarily counseling of souls in the way of perfection."[24] Eventually, under the Dominicans lay persons were trained as spiritual directors and women religious began to receive direction.[25]

Another great religious educator, Gerard Groote (1340-1384), stressed obedience to superiors as a fundamental part of his spiritual direction. Thomas a Kempis, one of the greatest products of Groote's *devotic moderna,* placed great importance on spiritual direction as a way to obtain deep peace of soul. His devotional work, *Imitation of Christ*, became one of the most widely used spiritual guidebooks in Western Christianity—as it remains today. By the end of the twelfth century, spiritual direction began to move definitely outside the monastic environment and into the outside world through the Franciscan, the Dominican, and other mendicant orders.[26]

Seeking the Holy

Spiritual Direction Beyond the Middle Ages

The practice of spiritual direction suffered from the general corruption and moral decline of the Church in the Middle Ages. The Protestant Reformers rejected the practice of direction along with oral confession and all of the ". . . paraphernalia of piety assembled to guide the faithful in the Middle Ages.[27] As a result, the burden of spiritual direction fell heavily on the Reformers themselves. Luther, Calvin, and leaders in Puritanism and Pietism all practiced some form of spiritual direction.

> What fell by the wayside in Protestantism, however, was the availability of spiritual assistance for whoever would seek it. By the second generation the problem became acute, forcing the revival of many forms of medieval spirituality by Puritans in England and Pietists on the Continent.[28]

The Puritans' efforts at reformation in England brought about a renewal of ascetic and contemplative practices of the medieval monks (fasting, prayer, meditation on Scripture, including individual spiritual direction.[29]

For the Pietist religious educator August Hermann Francke (1664-1727), the express object of education was helping believers grow toward living an exemplary and intentional Christian life.[30] He regularly used small groups (sometimes referred to as "cell groups") as an approach for spiritual direction. These groups, composed of clergy and laypeople, gathered for Bible study, prayer, confession, and discernment. Francke's form of direction exerted a significant impact on Protestant spirituality through the Moravians, the Wesleys, and modern revivalism. "The Moravian cell group furnished John Wesley with a model for the Methodist class meetings which offered corporate spiritual direction."[31]

In early American Puritanism, spiritual direction was a common practice. The themes of conscience, self-examination, meditation, and conversation were evident in sermons and letters. The writings of such leaders as Thomas Booker, Increase and Cotton Mather, and Jonathan Edwards all encouraged lay Christians to give themselves to mutual admonition as well as to the personal cultivation of their souls.[32]

In the sixteenth century, the character of spiritual direction once again became institutionalized. The practice was given new life by the Counter Reformation, the Council of Trent, and through the works of such religious leaders as St. Ignatius of Loyola, St. Phillip Neri, and Frances de Sales. These religious leaders saw spiritual direction as a necessary correction to the neglect and decline of the Church in the previous epoch.[33]

Ignatius of Loyola's (1491-1556) classic *Spiritual Exercises* (1548), which encouraged the practice of individual and group retreats, contributed greatly to the resurgence of the practice of spiritual direction. Ignatius was able to combine the best of the monastic tradition of spiritual guidance with the demands of an educational institution. His program continues to dominate modern Catholic spirituality and formation, and has found acceptance in Protestant faiths.

At the heart of Ignatius' spiritual direction was his insistence on the absolute necessity of a spiritual director's complete authority over the person receiving guidance. The discernment of spirits is central to the spiritual direction of Ignatius. Through discernment both the director and the directee are able to safely journey into the spiritual life. "The pattern of the devout life was to involve daily meditation, daily examination of conscience, weekly confession and communion, open confession to a good confessor, spiritual reading and fellowship with other Christians, and daily growth is virtues."[34] Ignatius' direction was characterized by discernment, common sense, methodology, service, reason, love, and stern discipline.[35]

A contemporary of Ignatius, St. Philip of Neri, began around the same time to practice spiritual direction intensely. The practice was essential to his apostolate, and he gave direction with ". . . profound perception being at the same time paternal and firm."[36] In Spain, meanwhile, Teresa of Avila (1515-1582) and St. John of the Cross (1543-1591) were aiding in the renewal of the Church through spiritual direction. St. Teresa gave special attention to the qualifications of the spiritual director. As a noted religious educator, she regarded theological learning as a fundamental qualification in a spiritual educator, ". . . no less necessary than a personal experience of spiritual things." [37]

St. John of the Cross also gave special attention to the needs and qualifications of the spiritual director. He closely linked direction to the life of the Church as it related to the soul's journey toward perfection in the Holy Spirit. Like many of the spiritual directors, surveyed here, Teresa and John of the Cross lamented the lack of competent spiritual directors, and were harshly critical of incompetent and inadequately prepared directors.[38]

The Golden Age of Spiritual Direction

The seventeenth century is considered by many historians to be the golden age of spiritual direction.[39] Some of the richest literature on the subject of spiritual direction emerged during this period. Direction took on the characteristics of being continuous with sacraments, including confession and bearing close resemblance to monastic direction. During this time spiritual direction was practiced not only by the religious orders, but many lay individuals (both men and women) became famous for their skills as spiritual directors.[40]

St. Francis de Sales (1567-1622) was the leading spiritual director of the period as is evident in his *Introduction to the Devout Life*, the most complete teaching regarding direction until this time. Typical of the period, his spiritual direction took place in the context of sacramental confession, but he also stressed friendship in the direction relationship. Because of this, the process of direction took on a more reciprocal character than previously. Under de Sales' direction, directees enjoyed a major role in discerning God's will for their lives. Studzinski described de Sales' approach in direction:

De Sales paid attention to people's feelings and appealed to them as a means of strengthening the will in its quest for God. He would elicit positive feelings not only toward such things as the suffering of Christ but also toward himself as minister and friend as a way of drawing people toward God. This affective method was indicative of De Sales' genius. It contributed to his success in drawing the whole person into the sphere of God's merciful love.[41]

The Contemporary Resurgence of Spiritual Direction

Though spiritual direction continued in quiet ways and in different forms during the eighteenth and nineteenth centuries, it was not until the twentieth century that it experienced a resurgence of interest and practice. This was due in part to new projects in editing old spiritual texts, the publishing of contemporary journals dedicated to spiritual direction and formation, and to the encouragement received from Pope Pius III in 1950 for the practice of direction.[42] The findings of depth psychology have given the practice of direction new tools and insights into guiding the individual in his spiritual life. Spiritual directors found new vitality given to their ancient practice in depth psychology's attention to the psychic realities of man's being and to necessity of symbolic language in interpreting human experience.[43]

While there has been a resurgence of spiritual direction in the Catholic Church and in higher Protestant traditions, this has been, until recently, much slower in most Protestant denominations. As Hinson pointed out, from the time of the Great

Awakening onward, ". . . personal spiritual guidance became increasingly casual and superficial as Protestant memories of earlier traditions in spiritual direction faded away."[44] Gerald G. May suggested one reason for this, claiming that for Protestants,

> . . . there have often been special theological problems with the idea of one person advising another in intimate matters of the spirit. Much of the concern here has to do with sacerdotalism, the possibility that the methods or personality of the spiritual director would surplant the role of Jesus as the prime mediator between God and the individual human being. Thus Protestants have characteristically tended to rely more on group spiritual guidance in faith-sharing meetings and on the private experience of prayer and personal scripture reflection .[45]

May suggested that the emphasis on psychology and counseling in the pastoral care of Protestantism stems from a lack of tradition in formal spiritual direction. He observed that while there is a currant movement toward traditional spiritual direction, ". . . Protestants have almost not tested and accepted methods of individual spiritual direction. . . ."[46] This is slowly changing as evidenced in the increasing acceptance of direction among Protestant traditions and the proliferation of programs in spiritual formation as well as training in spiritual direction.

Certain elements and characteristics of spiritual direction are evident from the above historical survey. First, it becomes evident that spiritual direction has had many forms throughout the centuries. The practice has been seen as "the cure of souls," closely tied to pastoral care and confession, but at other times, it was seen as a distinct discipline. Spiritual direction has been the province of both professional clergy and of lay persons. At times, great emphasis was placed on the training of the spiritual guide, while at other times, the simple element of friendship was seen as most important. Formal spiritual direction has centered on a number of elements: the seeking of the Holy, the intimate journey into self and spirit (St. John of the Cross and Teresa of Avila), the discernment of spirits (Ignatius of Loyola), or psychological growth, individualism, self-actualization (modern depth-psychology approaches).

Second, a major characteristic of spiritual direction throughout its history was that it was focused on the formation of the clergy or religious. This fostered an idea of a separate life of the Spirit, a distinctly religious life contrasted with (sometimes opposed to) a secular lifestyle. Third, spiritual direction usually has been characterized by a subservient relationship to the director, at times even an authoritarian relationship, though an occasional voice raised the ideal of spiritual friendship in direction. Fourth, developmental psychology and stage theories have raised the idea of definite and definable normative stages of spiritual growth in the life of the individual, prompting directors to give greater attention to developmental issues.

> Throughout the history of spiritual direction, enormous energy and imagination have been used to depict the stages of spiritual growth. Catholic mystics travel a well-worn, well-known path through the dark night of the

senses and of the soul. Progress in prayer, for example, moves from discursive prayer to meditation, from meditation to contemplation and—for the advanced in the spiritual life—to the mystic marriage, and finally, the union.[47]

Fifth, throughout its history spiritual direction has been closely linked to religious education. Many of the spiritual directors surveyed above were recognized religious educators: Jesus, Paul, Francis, Teresa, Groote, Ignatius, Augustine, Luther, Calvin, Wesley. Sixth, there historically has been a continual resistance on the part of Protestants in accepting many key elements of the practice of spiritual direction. They tended to react against the sacramental and sacerdotal overtones as well as well as the more mystical elements of direction. The cure of souls took on a different character in Protestant life, paradoxically more corporate in some contexts and more individualistic in others. In contemporary Protestant life, psychology and clinical counseling seem to have substituted for spiritual direction for a time. Today there is evidence of a rediscovery and resurgence of the practice of spiritual direction among Protestant faith traditions.

The Practice of Spiritual Direction in a Psychological Age

As mentioned there is an increased interest in the practice of spiritual direction today, even in Protestant denominations. Edwards identified two possible reasons for this renewed interest.

First, Edwards claimed that there is a felt need for personal growth in a "Christian way of life."[48] This is so especially in the context of a lack of a clear spiritual worldview within and outside the church. Second, there is a growing sense of limitations in traditional educational programs and interpersonal relationships which ignore the spiritual dimension of the adult.

Sociologists Josh Packard and Ashleigh Hope's alarming book, *Church Refugees: Sociologists Reveal Why People Are DONE With Church But Not Their Faith,* provide evidence of several factors why traditional educational programs and congregational structures may cause people to "leave church" in search of spiritual fulfillment elsewhere. Among the reasons are a need for a sustaining spiritual community, intimate and meaningful conversation, and meaningful engagement in the world. While these are the things faithful and committed Christians desire of their churches, say Packard and Hope, they receive other things instead (judgement, bureaucracy, doctrine, and moral prescriptions)—everything but an experience of the Holy.[49]

Psychologists, as well as sociologists, claims Edwards, see the need for a more authentically spiritual engagement in the life of persons. Edwards claims there is and increasing attention among therapists in

> ... transpersonal and Jungian therapists and in Eastern (and to some extent Western) mystical traditions to this hunger. Though the quest is veiled in psychological language, and usually is limited to intrapsychic

investigation. I sense in many of them a yearning for a transcendently rooted way of life.[50]

In the next chapter, a clearer picture of the distinctiveness of spiritual direction will emerge by comparing and contrasting spiritual direction with other types and forms of pastoral care, counseling, and therapy. One of the difficulties in the area of the practice of spiritual direction (or the lack of it), is the fact that most of the people given responsibility for the care of souls today, that is, religious professionals, have increasingly been ". . . given much the same kind of training and assumptions about human development as the mental-health professional . . . ."[51] Barry and Connolly have pointed out that with the emergence of modern theories of therapy and counseling, pastoral care has ". . . too often looked like a carbon copy of these secular models."[52] Jean Laplace cautioned his readers on the overdependence on psychology for spiritual growth and formation, stating that the focus and technique of spiritual direction lie elsewhere.[53]

Harville Hendrix, at the 1976 convention of the American Association of Counselors, voiced his concerns of the effects this trend has had in pastoral counseling. He contended that pastoral counselors need to learn from the tradition of spiritual direction how to help people resolve the human problem.[54] Barry argued that spiritual direction is the form of pastoral care from which all other forms of pastoral counseling radiate.[55]

Despite the concern of spiritual directors about the overdependence on secular models and psychologies, there is also newfound acceptance of the need and mutual dependence of the disciplines of spiritual direction and psychology and counseling. Most writers on spiritual direction stress the need for knowledge of the psychological disciplines on the part of the spiritual director.[56] Alan Jones suggested that in many religious circles, ". . . we have suffered from a form of spirituality that has repressed the awful knowledge which the psychoanalytic revolution has brought us."[57] An understanding of psychology contributes to an integrated understanding of the life span and the methods and means for dealing with all dimensions of the adult's life situations, inclusive of mind, psyche, and spirit.

> Our religions strivings, practices and attitudes are often all mixed up with authority and sexual problems, as well as with anxiety neuroses and other psychological problems. I doubt if either the religious or psychological dimensions of life can be dealt with adequately without a knowledge of the other.[58]

Psychoanalyst Carl Jung's relevance to the practice of spiritual direction is substantial. Jung stressed that psychological healing could not take place without spiritual healing. Many of the methods used by Jung in his practice were much the same as found and taught in Ignatian direction. For example, Jung accepted liturgical worship and prayer as key elements in the process of individuation, as is in spiritual direction.[59]

CHAPTER 2

Spiritual Direction, Counseling, and Therapy

Obviously, since spiritual direction, psychotherapy, and pastoral counseling all deal with personality and human experience there is an overlap in their practices. The practice of spiritual direction is not indifferent to emotional difficulties or developmental arrests in the person.[60] Like counseling, spiritual direction at times is crisis-centered. In spiritual direction, however, these issues are seen as intimately related to the process of integration by the religiously- or spiritually-oriented adult. This chapter reviews the similarities and contrasts between the helping professions of spiritual direction, counseling, and therapy.

Similarities Between Direction and Counseling

Both spiritual direction and counseling deal with the person in a holistic manner, not in a compartmentalized approach.[61] Leech suggested three examples of the inter-relationship between spiritual and psychological progress: 1) self-discovery is necessary for emotional maturity; 2) attention to the physical body is important for spiritual and psychological health; 3) there is a need to ". . . travel the way of the unconscious in order to recover the awareness of God."[62] Both spiritual direction and psychology specifically address these integrated domains.

Like psychotherapy, spiritual direction is interested in understanding the life history, thoughts, hopes, and feelings of the adult. Both disciplines give attention to the nature of the personal relationships of the individual, past and present. Both disciplines are concerned with enabling the adult to come to terms with aspects of the past which hinder growth in the present or make mature relationships problematic.[63] Both direction and counseling contain a didactic dimension when there is need to provide clarification, simple instruction, and correction of factual knowledge.[64]

Both spiritual direction and psychotherapy depend on the motivation of the adult who comes for help. The reasons why people seek spiritual direction are varied and parallel those of counseling and therapy, including crises of self, a sense of a divided self and the need for integration, ego-desperation, feelings of restlessness, a search for meaning, and the need for increased self-awareness about one's internal state and the relationships that sustain or block living fully.[65] These motivations tend to be particular to the second half of life as many are emergent tensions and issues related to maturation and spiritual development.

Another similarity between psychotherapy and spiritual direction is their provision for training in decision-making, or, more particularly for spiritual direction, the development of discernment. Both disciplines strive to make the person more aware of his or her unconscious self by bringing it to conscious awareness in order to facilitate rational life choices.[66] In spiritual direction, this process is traditionally called discernment. "Like the psychotherapeutic techniques, discernment results in a better knowledge of the self and the various influences which affect the self."[67]

From the above discussion, it is easy to deduce that spiritual direction and psychotherapy have similar goals. Gratton has pointed out that the shift in the goals of psychotherapies to a more holistic dialogical attention to the meaning of the person's problem has resulted in a blurring of the lines that traditionally divided ". . . therapy from spiritual guidance, psychological practice from sacred tradition."[68] Some of the emerging goals of psychotherapy that parallel the unique realm of spiritual direction include: attention to cultivating a meditative presence, the practice of reflective living, an appreciation for transcendence, a search for meaning, and authenticity of being."[69]

One final significant similarity between the disciplines under discussion needs to be mentioned. Jones articulated this similarity well, and it has been echoed by psychologists (like Jung, Rogers, and Fromm) and directors as well: "For both therapist and director, insofar as each is participating in a double process of healing and of growth, love is the supreme requirement."[70]

Contrasting Direction and Counseling

So then, the helping disciplines of psychotherapy, pastoral counseling and spiritual direction have much in common. Seemingly, it may appear that pastoral counseling, or even some forms of therapy, is in effect merely a contemporary form of spiritual direction. In fact, Edwards suggested that one reason for the neglect of spiritual direction has been the rise of humanistic and developmental psychologies in this century.[71]

But writers and practitioners in the discipline of spiritual direction caution that psychology and counseling have real limitations in the dimension of spiritual development. Jones, for example, claimed that modern therapy, at its best, can only help prepare a person for a deeper and a more wonderful engagement with life by removing internal obstacles.[72] This is done largely (to use a gross over-simplification) by giving emphasis to a person's consciousness and appealing to an intellectual, cognitive mastery over the subconscious and/or emotions. But Edwards noted that what the ancient literature of spiritual direction demonstrated was the primacy of ". . . firsthand spiritual awareness and humble, purifying loving in the spiritual life, for which no intellectual mastery can substitute."[73]

As a result of the loss of attention to the uniqueness of spiritual direction, and due to a lack of a tradition in spiritual direction especially among Protestant circles, and as a result of the noted rise of psychology,

> the price has been a tragic Western categorization of the truth into bits and pieces that never seem to weave a single cloth. In mainline churches, for example, theologians offer broad scale analysis. Helping a person with the integral appropriation of the truth to which theology points, however, is left to "practical" people, especially pastoral clergy. Unable adequately to translate their theological training into the nitty-gritty of the personal crises and developmental help asked of them by people, and goaded by the lack of perceived spiritual concerns on the part of many people coming for help. . . they usually turn to the empirical sciences for assistance. In terms of practical human guidance, this has bred clinical pastoral education and the pastoral counselor.[74]

Gratton pointed out that typical pastoral counselors lack a holistic, unified foundational orientation in their practice. Schooled in theology and coming from a religious background and world view, their formal clinical training tends not to be very profound ". . . and may well consist of a fairly eclectic amalgam of Freudian, Jungian, transactional, gestalt and a variety of other theories."[75]

Overreliance on the psychological disciplines can result in a tendency to become abstract and remote in the helping situation. This may happen, for example, in the exclusive use of psychological language to describe the person's situation or difficulty ("affective underdevelopment," "identity crisis," "inability to achieve psychic intimacy," "oppositional defiant disorder," etc.). Barry and Connolly pointed out that though the use of clinical terminology may accurately describe the person's predicament, they do not adequately represent what may be the most important dimension of all: the unresolved issues related to the spiritual relationship of the person with God.[76] Practitioners of spiritual direction are of the conviction that in order to address the spiritual dimensions of the adult, the kind of guidance needed is more than merely psychological. In terms of practice, it can be claimed that theological language must be use to address theological concerns; and, the language of spirituality must be used to interpret issues of the spirit.

Differences Between Spiritual Direction and Counseling and Therapy

Clearly, spiritual direction has much in common with pastoral counseling and psychotherapy. Further, spiritual direction has benefited from the insights and techniques found in those disciplines. But there are unique dimensions in the practice of spiritual direction that give it a significant distinctiveness. For one thing, though a crisis situation may have been the initiator of the person seeking direction, the relationship between director and directee continues after the immediate problem is solved. This is because in spiritual direction there is concern with the larger issues of continued growth and development.[77] A crisis of the soul is not something to be "fixed" and from which a person "moves on." Spiritual crises are nodal events and part of a process of movements that involve transitions, detours on the journey, and alerts that the soul requires attention. Crises of the spirit may be gateways to liminal epochs that challenge persons toward a choice for growth or stagnation.

While spiritual direction gives attention to the past and present orientation of the individual with the corresponding effects in his or her life, there is a more transcendent orientation in that it looks from the present to the future—even beyond hope in death. In spiritual direction there is an attempt to discover a unique meaning in the individual's life structure ". . . whose source is God and which leads to full religious and human development through deliberate choices in the here and now."[78] There is in spiritual direction a very deliberate attempt to interpret the person's experience of life and living in the context of faith.

In the process of spiritual direction there tends to be a more relaxed and up-front atmosphere in which there is focus on the way grace is operating in the life of the directee. With the spiritual director, the directee seeks to discover how grace is accepted, resisted, and being responded to in prayer and action.[79] In this context, the directee, unlike the client in a counseling or clinical therapy relationship, participates actively in a mutually accepted approach to a reality represented by Christian faith.[80]

This attention to the salient feature of faith in the life of the person, and between the director and directee, is unique to the practice of spiritual direction. The difference between spiritual direction and counseling or therapy, therefore, is not so much in practice or technique, they can appear similar, but in the faith orientation of both the director and the directee.[81] Dyckman referred to this shared faith dimension as fidelity to the Gospel—by which she meant, in effect, faithfulness to the shared, mutual relationship with Christ.[82] This shared faith affects the whole helping relationship and centers it on Christ. With this shared faith-context, the aims of the spiritual direction experience takes on a particular dimension.

> As a director we are not just enabling people to reflect on and integrate life, as any good counselor would do, but to do so in the light of 'who they are called to become in fidelity to the Gospel.' This meeting with Jesus in faith is the decided and distinct difference between counseling and spiritual direction.[83]

When faith is accepted as the central domain of the spiritual life, the capacity for religious experiences (mystical, emotional, or mundane) become a secondary concern, so that "neither spiritual director nor directee need to be mystics or experts in religious experiencing.[84]

This focus on faith is the key difference that highlights the distinctiveness of spiritual direction. As Gordon E. Jackson claimed, ". . . the most critical problem in contemporary pastoral care and counseling [is] the missing element of God."[85] Spiritual direction is concerned with seeing the totality of the person's life in the light of God's redemptive relationship with God's creation. In this perspective one's total world includes God as well, ". . . . and that the Spirit of God is trying to share God's life with each person."[86] In effect, spiritual direction goes beyond seeking solutions of our problems, it is, in effect, seeking the Holy.

Spiritual direction is also attentive to one of the central concerns of Christianity: the dynamic of change through conversion, the radical transformation of the person in Christ. Conversion, or *metanoia*, is never a matter of an exclusively cognitive activity, a changing from one belief system to another, or an assent to a certain set of beliefs. Rather, it is a relational, personal surrender to a personal, living God.[87] For Jones, this is the difference between spiritual direction and secular therapy, ". . . this explicit commitment to Jesus. It is in him that we find out who we really are."[88] Again, in spiritual direction this *metanoia* is the concern at the center of the person's whole life and not restricted to a perceived exclusive or abstract spiritual realm.[89]

This dimension of *metanoia* gives rise to another distinction between spiritual direction and psychotherapy. The reference point for evaluating the results and benefits of counseling and therapy lies in the human social arena: the needs, wishes, and goals of the individual, and, the social requirements of the community and society. In spiritual direction, however, the reference point for evaluation is in the directee's relationship with God and his or her participation in the shared corporate life of Christian community, the church.[90]

Seeking the Holy

Most significant in this regard is the fact that therapy and counseling do not provide ". . . an ongoing community to sustain the person through a period of upheaval."[91] The experiences of heightened awareness that come as a result of the crises in the second half of life, and which are part of the process of integration and individuation, may leave the adult feeling perplexed and dissatisfied with life circumstances, work, and relationships. Jones asserted that a breakthrough in insight into the soul may not make much sense to the adult unless ". . . there is an interpreter or companion and unless it happens within the broadening context of a worshiping community.[92] Spiritual direction brings to bear more of the resources of the body of Christ into the life of the adult than does even individual pastoral counseling, which has come to be separated from the common life of the local church.[93] As Leech phrased the shortcoming, ". . . the counseling movement has been clinic-based rather than church-based or community-based."[94]

A major difference between spiritual direction and counseling or therapy is that spiritual direction deals primarily with the healthy individual, rather than pathologies. Attending to deep psychiatric problems lie outside the boundaries of the practice of spiritual direction.[95] Spiritual direction is more the province of adults who ". . . seek <u>coherence</u> and <u>communion</u>, a renewed meaning to their lives, and a deepening relationship with the source of their being."[96] For this reason, the experience of spiritual direction is especially suited to the developmental period of the second half of life. The emphasis in the direction relationship is on

35

growth motivation rather than deficiency remediation, and goes beyond functional living to ". . . optimal Christian living."[97] According to Jones, therapy and counseling cannot provide the answers to those questions of meaning and purpose for which the adult in the second half of life longs.[98] But spiritual direction, in the context of relationship, community, conversion, and faith, can help the adult with those existential dimensions of their journey during the second half of life.

Unlike the helping situations of counseling and therapy, there is a prerequisite need for a level of maturity and self-knowledge on the part of the adult in spiritual direction.[99] In this sense, spiritual direction is not suited to everyone. Some adults, because of emotional or psychological immaturity, will not be able to take full advantage of the distinct dynamics offered in spiritual direction. Persons in "lower" stages of faith as described in the work of James Fowler—those below Stage 4—will not likely benefit fully from direction. The structure of faith and the framework of meaning making in those stages do not equip the person for the work of direction.[100] Spiritual direction will be of minimal help to those who are incapable or unwilling to engage in an honest, critical, introspective journey into their spiritual lives, qualities that are rare in stages of faith below Stages 4 or 5. Spiritual direction will help best those adults who are able and willing to raise questions

> . . . which come from the depth of a person's being. They spring from a deep concern that religious fidelity is not

getting his or her anywhere or that it has not resulted in a sense of peace and integration.[101]

The Source of Spiritual Direction

Perhaps the fundamental difference between spiritual direction and the helping professions of counseling and therapy has to do with what is considered the "source" of spiritual direction. There is in spiritual direction a fundamental assumption that God wants to relate to, and communicate, with God's people as community and as individuals.[102] Spiritual direction is ultimately the work of the Holy Spirit; the practice, experience, and relationship of direction provides a context for the experiencing of God's grace.[103] In the context of spiritual direction God is seen as the source of spiritual experience, something that has been neglected even in contemporary pastoral counseling.[104]

No modern writer on spiritual direction has improved on the words of St. John of the Cross concerning the Spirit as the source of direction:

> The Holy Spirit is the principle agent and mover of souls and never loses care for them; and the directors themselves are not agents but only instruments to lead souls . . . is the rule of faith and is the law of God according to the spirituality that God is giving to each one.[105]

This unique demonstration of spiritual direction raises an important epistemological issue, namely, the belief that God is active in communicating with the individual in context of relationships and community. Part of the process of spiritual direction is the bringing of people to a new level of awareness. The process brings people into a new and larger perspective of God's presence under the Spirit's guidance.[106] This different spiritual reality, considered perhaps mystical, is what Paul spoke of in Ephesians 1:18-19: an awareness of the invisible presence of Christ in the formation of the person. In Paul's view,

> . . . the initiative for this new view of reality is ultimately not to be found in the effort and good will of either . . . teacher and learner, counselor or client . . . but is actually a gift of the Father's merciful love that brings people back to life in Christ at the very moment when they are dead to this life through sin.[107]

This epistemological view provides the understanding that the world of the Spirit is a world largely of mystery, ". . . operating very much out of a quite different set of realities then we are accustomed to is this world."[108] The basic assumptions in spiritual direction, then, grow out of the conviction that God operates in the world in God's own way. With this distinct view of reality comes the realization and acceptance that many people are genuinely touched by supernatural and spiritual dimensions in the course of living their lives.[109] As such, in spiritual direction, religious experiences are accepted as more normative than in clinical therapeutic contexts.

Jones contended that psychology (and the type of pastoral counseling practiced in contemporary churches) cannot help adults in choosing the direction of spiritual growth or discernment in matters of the Spirit; for this, psychology is inadequate. He said,

> We need to be rescued from the damaging reductionist tendency that wishes to explain everything in psychological terms. The psychologist has infected the Church and, in particular, the important field of pastoral counseling.[110]

As Gratton explained, some things in the spiritual dimension cannot be quantified or explained in psychological frames of reference.[111] In spiritual direction there is the conviction that the mysteries of faith have a healing power within themselves.[112]

The Spirit, as the source of spiritual direction, also serves to integrate the breach between the psychological and spiritual dimensions that, as Jung demonstrated, inhibits the integration of the self. The practice of spiritual direction allows for no false division between sacred and profane dimensions in the life of the believer.[113]

> If it is seen and believed that it is the Holy Spirit himself who is the director, that it is he who undergirds human life, growth, and potential, then two things happen; psychology is put in its place (vital but subordinate) and the Holy Spirit is accepted as the real initiator and creator of human life and community.[114]

With the understanding that the Holy Spirit is the source of direction and is the 'real' director in the spiritual direction relationship, then the context of spiritual direction (as opposed to that of psychotherapy) becomes focused on the practices of prayer, adoration, worship, liturgy, and grace.[115] Grace, in this context, is the working of the Spirit in the life of the directee to change and transform.[116] In the practice and experience of direction it is expected that the Spirit's transforming power comes as much in common and ordinary ways in all areas of the adult's life, as in the extraordinary and experientially religious.[117]

CHAPTER 3

The Goals of Spiritual Direction

In this chapter we will identify more precisely the aims and goals of spiritual direction as it becomes possible within the context of the understanding that the Holy Spirit is the source of transformative spiritual development in spiritual direction.

Spiritual Growth

First of all, the goal of spiritual direction lies in affecting spiritual growth in the day-to-day reality of the believer, not in ". . . the supernatural manifestations of ecstasy.[118] This is only biblical, for the Apostle Paul stressed that a person's spirituality is not divided from personal daily experiences of incarnation and participation, of interpersonal relations, of manual work and leisure, of sexuality and prayer (see Ephesians 6). Neither is it separated from ". . . all the difficulties, disappointments, losses and heartaches that this existence inevitably involves."[119]

Vanderwall described the spiritual condition of many adults in the second half of life that illustrates the need for spiritual direction. He said, ". . . deep down inside us, unspoken perhaps but nevertheless experienced, we know that there is more, much more than the superficiality of the daily grind, and we long for the depths of our beings to be evoked so that the deep within us may be united to the deep of God."[120]

Union With God

A second distinct and clear goal of spiritual direction is to lead people to that which most deeply meets their needs: to union with God in Christ through the Holy Spirit.[121] This union with God involves all aspects of the person's life and is the end goal in seeking the Holy.

Union with God makes possible for believers ways to hear and cooperate with the voice of the Spirit that is in them, and permits the realization of God's will in their lives.

> Outside of crisis times, over the long haul of life, the director enables a person to see rhythm and patterns, to discern what past decisions led to deeper union with the Lord or to more freedom with others. In the midst of a deepening interpersonal relationship the director becomes progressively more able to indicate the moods and moves that make the directee feel and be more authentic.[122]

This has direct application to adult needs in the second half of life, for achieving a sense of meaning to their lives and to examine and readjust the life structure created over time to this point in their lives.

Discernment

Another fundamental goal of spiritual direction, which is resurgent in significant ways for adults in the second half of life, is that of discernment. "The basis of discernment of spirits is the undoubted fact that temptations, errors and illusions are commonly encountered on the spiritual path."[123] Traditional Christian teaching on the spiritual life has often included the movements of the spirits and ways of finding God's will in the choices one makes in life. At its most basic level, discernment consists of recognizing differences, knowing what is, and what isn't.[124] Though discernment is a simple process at heart, it is not always an easy one to achieve.

Self-Knowledge

Three other goals of spiritual direction have great significance for the adults in the second half of life. First, spiritual direction has as a goal to help persons achieve a deeper level of self-knowledge.[125] This self-knowledge is a direct result of the previous mentioned goal of discernment. Self-knowledge comes through discovering all parts of the self (in Jung's terms, conscious and unconscious, shadow and light, masculine and feminine) as they relate to God and to one's relationship with God. This self-knowledge comes, in part, as the person moves away from an overly intellectualized or rationalistic faith to a more affective appreciation of faith, self, and God. For adults in the second half of life, giving attention to their feelings and emotions can be the basis for sound discernment regarding their own conversions.[126] This is significant to spiritual development, for as Sudbrack noted, coming to terms with oneself successfully is the key to the spiritual life.[127]

There is little capacity for a deep spiritual life for the person without self-acceptance, self-worth, or centeredness. A large part of spiritual direction is guiding persons to find their own center.[128] In spiritual direction persons come to a deeper affective self-knowledge that is essential to the conversion processes particular to the second half of life.[129]

Self-knowledge is the first requisite to encountering the shadow, which as Jung pointed out, is necessary for the integration of the self.[130] In terms of spiritual development, recognition of the shadow leads to an acknowledgement, and acceptance, of one's imperfection, or in more theological terms, one's sinfulness. Growth in the spiritual life necessitates the ". . . striving to know and to accept oneself and others in the strengths and weaknesses that each possesses."[131]

Knowledge of one's shadow (sinfulness) allows for a new *metanoia*, a " . . . surrender of the self to rediscover ourselves in Christ."[132] Through conversion comes the freedom that results from accepting oneself as a forgiven sinner. A sense of personal freedom is essential to spiritual growth and for successful spiritual direction.[133]

> It often seems to us that one of the simplest and yet most significant things a director does is to help people recognize these truths and accept themselves. They then know that God accepts them, along with their strong emotions....[134]

The process of self-knowledge in spiritual direction correlates well with the movement toward interiority during the second half of life, as identified by Neugarten, Jung, and others. In the context of spiritual direction, however, self-awareness is given a specific focus, and its distinction comes in "... the difference between the relatively isolated self-knowledge that results from a merely psychological approach to self-awareness by means of introspection, and the knowledge of self-in-relation-to-mystery that comes with meditative reflection on that same self as loved by God."[135]

Integration

The second goal of spiritual direction that is most relevant for adult spiritual development is the integration of the individual as identified by Jung.

> The aim of the process of self-knowledge in spiritual direction correlates well with the interiority of mid-life identified by Neugarten, Jung, and others. It is the achievement of wholeness of life, an integrated personality, in which the inner and the outer [person] are united. Yet to become whole and integrated is painful, it is a process which involves conflict and crisis, and all spiritual direction is involved in the crisis of the soul.[136]

Jung gave great emphasis to the role of religion in the process of individuation. The symbol systems of religion offered the means, in Jung's view, for the integration of all parts of reality into a meaningful whole, ". . . one to which the individual psyche could be related."[137] In spiritual direction a main task is that of helping the individual integrate his or her life into the meaning that his or her highest ritual symbolizes.[138]

> The directee discovers that God is in his or her life, guiding, sustaining, and leading to a fuller integration of self. While time is spent discussing the directee's prayer and religious thought, the direction process is holistic, and no dimension of a person's life is irrelevant to it.[139]

Generativity

A final goal of spiritual direction that is especially relevant to spiritual development in the second half of life is one that can be termed spiritual generatively. Spiritual direction is concerned with a person's calling and mission in light of her or his underlying discovery of self, God, and the promptings of the Spirit.[140] Spiritual direction aims at helping the directees to share with others in their individual need the love and compassion that God has effected in their own lives. In direction, the person comes to understand that self-acceptance and care for others is interdependent, the more a person affirms himself in an authentic relationship with God the more he or she can serve others.[141]

Faith is primarily a corporate human quality, though it has authentic individual, and personal, dimensions. As there is no self apart from community, spiritual direction addresses not only interior experiences of the individual, but also the larger social matrix of relationships of a person's life. In the practice of spiritual direction, a maturing adult faith is not possible without a freely chosen and felt sense of social order which is neither ". . . simply 'selling out' to prevailing cultural values nor an overenthusiastic idealism which cannot commit itself within a real social context."[142]

Helping adults grow in their spiritual life in the context of spiritual direction involves helping them to care about and for others. This includes helping the directee discover areas of the self which one is able to use in generative ways. According to Whitehead and Whitehead, "Christian service or *diakonia* is better understood as one grasps the complex challenge in generatively learning to care with others without controlling them.[143]

CHAPTER 4

The Process of Spiritual Direction

There are particular elements central to the experience of and process of spiritual direction. The process of spiritual direction is a journey in seeking the Holy. In this chapter we will review six elements in the process of spiritual direction.

Religious Experiences

First, as previously stated, religious experiences are a central concern in spiritual direction. Without religious experiences, there can be no spiritual direction.[144] This is a difficult matter to many, because the nature of religious experiences is that they are more a matter of apprehension than of comprehension.[145] What spiritual direction has demonstrated is that there is a need for a personal firsthand understanding of spirituality, one that comes through the experience of the Holy. Religious experiences go beyond the usual fare of achieving an intellectual, didactic, or propositional understanding of religious truths.[146]

In spiritual direction the effort is made to foster a different view of reality where the person can come to see that religious experiences take on many forms and shapes—common and unusual. The attempt is to read situations ". . . in terms of God's actions within people, of grace as a dynamic operative in human life which leads to greater love and service."[147] In the process of direction the directee learns to tell his or her story of faith, the narrative of meaning, in the context of religious experience.

Focusing on religious experiences, however, can be a risky venture. As much as personal religious experiences are legitimized as a normative part of one's spirituality, correctives to deviant subjective experiences must be provided. As much as religious experiences are a primary focus in spiritual direction, there is a need for objective criteria. In spiritual direction, religious experiences are evaluated against the criteria of the fruits of the Spirit and their positive redemptive evidence in the life of the directee.[148] "The quality of these criteria should be emphasized. They are positive fruits. They lead to an enduring sense of basic well-being."[149] Kelsey warned of the dangers of uncritical acceptance of religious experiences, saying that mystical and religious experiences need to be

> . . . . subjected to the same kind of analysis, comparison and understanding as any other experience if we are to grow religiously. When we leave behind our rationality and critical judgment, mysticism can become superstitious nonsense or silly experiences.[150]

Contemplation

A second major element in the process of spiritual direction is contemplation. Contemplation is the attitude or state of mind that leads to an experience of transcendence—of forgetfulness of self in the moment. Contemplation begins when the person stops being totally preoccupied with his or her own self and concerns and lets something or someone else have his or her total attention.[151] In terms of religious experience, contemplation ". . . means simply that we have a growing but unconscious (or unselfconscious) awareness of the reality of God and our oneness with [the Holy.]"[152] This attitude, often called detachment in the literature of spiritual direction, is of particular importance to the spiritual development of the adult in the second half of life. The detachment that is the result of contemplation manifests itself in growing trust, patience, and an ability to engage in religious generatively.[153]

Psychologists and therapists have demonstrated that if adults cannot reflect on the immediacy of their daily lives, they remain locked into habitual fixations and illusions of self and world.[154] Jones identified the ability to reflect and contemplate even in moments of solitude as a requirement for spiritual growth.[155] Contemplation is necessary in moving from the rational to the more affective aspects of religious experiences. "When thought and reason are the only elements of religious life, God is dead as far as transformation is concerned.

This emphasis on the too often neglected affective side of the spiritual life finds expression in the method of contemplative Scripture reading, an approach which is not for the purpose of intellectually understanding the text better ("understanding," "comprehension" or "analysis"), but whose end is to know Christ better. In his *Spiritual Exercises,* Ignatius described the goal of the person engaged in contemplative reading of the Gospels as desiring ". . . an intimate knowledge of our Lord, who has become man for me that I may love Him more and follow Him more closely.[156] In spiritual direction, Scripture is treated as ". . . literature intended to teach people how to let it inspire their imaginations and enkindle their faith as it was written to do."[157] Vanderwall put it nicely by pointing out the importance of ". . . listening to one's feelings while pondering Scripture, for it is there that God speaks with a great eloquence."[158] In terms of faith seeking understanding, the contemplative reading of scripture involves "learning to let the Bible read me."

This approach to Scripture reading is a resource and means in the process of integration as identified by Jung. By contemplating on Scripture from within the affective domain, and by contemplating on the affective side of the self (one's 'heart'), people can discover an image of themselves as rooted in God.[159] In spiritual direction the environment is provided where the images of self, God, and shadow are brought into consciousness. This is very important to spiritual formation in adulthood during the second half of life, a time when the cognitive aspect of faith (which makes up the belief system) and the affective aspect of faith may remain unconscious aspects of the self. They may even be unstated, ambivalent, and at cross-purposes. In mid-life, both aspects of faith are upset, become disorganized, and demand re-evaluation.[160]

Jung showed how the symbol systems of religion help in the integration process. Adults in the second half of life, who are in the process of integration, are sacramental creatures, seeking the holy and living their faith through symbols and sacraments.[161] The contemplative practices fostered in spiritual direction typically use ritual and sacraments to open up other realities and religious experiences. As Martha Robbins put it, ". . . symbolic images can transmit healing and integrating energies that often give profound meaning to the individual's life and connect his or her to greater mystery."[162]

Prayer

Another essential component in the process of spiritual direction, which is also closely tied to the practice of contemplation, is prayer. The primary type of prayer experience fostered in spiritual direction is contemplative prayer, that is, it involves focusing on and listening to something or someone other than oneself.[163] The contemplative center of prayer, and indeed of all Christian life, is a conscious relationship with God. Spiritual direction fosters this by helping adults pay attention to God as God reveals the presence of the Holy, and, by helping the directee recognize his or her reactions then guiding the person to decide on their responses to God in the process of seeking the Holy.[164] Like spirituality itself, contemplative prayer is not extraordinary, "It is as earthly as muddy boots, and as much involved with everyday life."[165]

Dyckman and Carroll present the following presuppositions of prayer which operate in spiritual direction: 1) prayer is a radical response to life growing out of one's interaction with God; 2) there is no dichotomy between praying and living; 3) God initiates and sustains the process of the prayer relationship.[166] A major criterion for testing to see if a person is growing in one's spiritual life is to see if there is growth in the prayer relationship with God.[167]

Contemplative prayer in spiritual direction helps adults in in the second half of life engage in the integration process that is the emergent lifework at that stage of life. Through openness before God adults can come to an acceptance of all their feelings, including their dark side—the shadow.[168] Prayer in the context of spiritual direction is an opportunity for adults to come into contact with the negative images that pull them away from their true spiritual identity. "Directors view such (negative) experiences developmentally, since they are aware that pain and conflict are inevitable in any movement toward a more fully integrated life."[169] The process of prayer is closely tied in with the elements of symbol and integration as proposed by Jung.

In spiritual direction, prayer involves the belief that God is calling each adult to become an increasingly unique person in relationship to Jesus Christ.[170] For this reason, as adults mature in their spiritual life, prayer moves from abstractions to a sharper focus on the person of Jesus Christ.[171] Mature contemplative prayer moves beyond the immature dimension of subject-object to a personal, affective, relational I-Thou dimension as described by Martin Buber.[172]

Discernment

As reviewed in the previous chapter, one goal of spiritual direction is to foster discernment, a key element in both the process of spiritual direction and in spiritual formation. The discernment that is fostered in spiritual direction is of special significance to adults in the second half of life. Discernment and conversion are correlative activities. Conversion and discernment serve as key frames of references for understanding the spiritual concerns of adults in the second half of life.[173]

Studzinski pointed out that in mid-life conversion, the adult is constantly leaving a past behind in order to ". . . be open for something more. Conversion requires a person to discern what is to be left behind and what to be welcomed."[174] The process involves coming to terms with one's past—one's childhood demons, faulty notions, immature images, unrealistic expectations, suppressed rage, and shadow. Discernment also involves dealing with one's limitations in mid-life and facing them realistically in order to make healthy decisions for future growth. These processes of retrospection and discernment of future directions were clearly evident in the works of psychologists like Vaillant, Gould, Levinson, Neugarten, Jung, and others.

In spiritual direction discernment is always focused on God's action in the life of the adult and on what is the appropriate response to the action of God. "For the person in mid-life, the question is often 'What is God's invitation to me at this point in my life?" O'Collins warned of counterfeit destinations in the second journey. He spoke of the need for discernment for recognizing counterfeit destinations and for making right choices during the second half of life and its second journey.[175]

Similar to the understanding of spirituality developed in this study,

> Discernment . . . engages persons holistically, in their feelings, memories, and imaginings. Within the framework of general moral principles, discernment helps people to make specific judgments about moral actions which are consistent with their graced life stories and consistent with their community's tradition of acting in response to God's calling.[176]

Decision-making through discernment is different from a purely rational process as tends to be found in pastoral counseling or in therapy. The decision-making process which results from discernment is based on a religious experience of God and gives as much weight to intuition, affect, and promptings as it does rationalistic and analytical considerations.

Relationship

Central to the process of spiritual direction is dialogue, and dialogue implies personal relationship.[177] James Fowler and Daniel Levinson both highlighted the importance of a sponsor or mentor for personal and faith development. In fact, Fowler's account of the role of the sponsor is descriptive of the relationship in spiritual direction.

> The sponsor is one who walks with you; one who knows the path and can provide guidance. The sponsor is one who engenders trust and proves trustworthy in supporting you in difficult passages of turns. The sponsor may, as needed, confront you, insisting that difficult issues be faced and that self-deceptions or sloth be avoided. The sponsor or sponsoring community should be able to provide both models and experiences in education and spiritual direction that deepen and expand one's initial commitments and provide the nurture for strong and continuing growth.[178]

A common metaphor for the spiritual director is that of a midwife of grace.[179] This imagery acknowledges that the source of growth in spiritual direction is the Holy Spirit, not the director. The direction relationship presupposes a willingness on the part of the directee to submit to the judgment of another, however, the only authority the director has is the authority of a companion who belongs to the Lord and to his community.[180] Kelsey pointed out that in Western traditional spirituality the relationship between teacher and student is not one of inequality, but of mutual interchange and increasing trust, love, and openness.[181]

"The direction relationship aims to facilitate on-going conversion at mid-life," stresses Studzinski.[182] This is done in the context of trust—Erikson's first condition for personal and moral growth.[183] In this trusting relationship the persons in dialogue create an open space where they can tell their stories—being able to verbalize what they see, feel, and believe is happening in their spiritual development. A story in this context takes the form of life narrative, which includes acknowledging one's past, coming to a deeper understanding of self, and incorporating and developing neglected dimensions of the self.

The directee's telling of his or her story in spiritual direction presupposes that the director knows how to listen. In the spiritual direction process, active listening involves more than merely hearing; it includes confrontation, affirmation, active engagement, and teaching.[184] As they listen to their directee's stories, directors respond to the Spirit's presence and invite people to a fuller realization of themselves and a reaffirmation, if not a rediscovery, of the reality of God.

One of the most significant and unique aspects of the direction relationship is the conscious and determined effort to foster love—an element that may or may not be found in pastoral counseling and which is generally uncalled for in most forms of therapy. All writers on spiritual direction highlight the importance and significance of love in the process of spiritual direction.

Simon Weil stated that the only way human beings can relate to one another creatively is through love, and true love, she said, requires a miracle—an act of God.[185]

Studzinski highlighted the significance of love for mid-life adult spiritual development,

> The experience of genuine love which is dependable helps a directee to move forward into a life where freedom for the true self is achievable. In such a loving relationship the directee's move to self-acceptance with all his or her past failures and successes is facilitated. God's unconditional love for each individual is reflected in such a relationship.[186]

Community

Although the process of spiritual direction is primarily that of dialogue in a one-to-one relationship, the individual's broader community is not neglected. In spiritual direction it is recognized that it is impossible to come to a full development in one's spiritual life apart from community.[187] In terms of spiritual formation, everything that goes on in the church—one's community of faith—will have some bearing upon a person's spiritual development—for better or for worse.[188] According to Leech, in spiritual direction there is concern for ". . . the encounter with God, the process by which the human community and the individual human being are made one with the divine." [189]

Spiritual direction therefore, takes place in the context of a believing, supportive community. The context of community provides the element of a firmly grounded tradition. The faith community, with its attention to Tradition, provides the touchstone whereby the person in direction tries to make sense of heightened spiritual experiences and new religious awareness. Jones explained that,

> Christian discernment . . . requires Christian companionship because it involves us in the life of a discerning community. Criteria for discerning root causes of our complex impulses and desires begin to emerge when we immerse ourselves in the life of a believing community. The Christian fellowship is formed by its attentiveness to the Christian drama as it unfolds in the reading of the scriptures and the celebration of the liturgy.[190]

Conclusion

In this chapter, we reviewed the key components in the practice of spiritual direction. Special attention was given to the relevance of spiritual direction to the spiritual development of the adult in the second half of life. I earlier chapters we surveyed the a historical practice and development of spiritual direction. Spiritual direction has its roots in a monastic tradition which developed as a way of guiding Catholic Christians in their spiritual development. Throughout its history, spiritual direction took many forms under various capable and extraordinary leaders. The close affiliation between spiritual direction and religious educators is noteworthy, especially in light of the growing interest and practice of spiritual direction in the contemporary Christian search of the Holy.

Seeking the Holy

In spiritual direction there is a distinct epistemological assumption. An acknowledgement exists of a separate reality that comes from the fact that God is actively engaged in personal communication with individuals. In this context, the practice falls under the actual direction of the Holy Spirit. With these assumptions, some clear and distinct differences between pastoral counseling and therapy and the practice and process of spiritual direction were highlighted.

Here is a summary of key points that arise out of our study of the history and practice of spiritual direction:

1. In spiritual direction there is no separation between the sacred and profane in the life of the individual.
2. In spiritual direction there is concern for the integration of the individual's self
3. In spiritual direction there is attention to the person's need to find meaning in life. This is done through relationship, the process of sharing the narrative of one's experience of life—the story of one's journey of faith—and through contemplation, and prayer
4. In spiritual direction emphasis is given to the need of the person to engage in spiritual generatively.
5. In spiritual direction the practice of discernment helps the individual find meaning in life and vocation—discovering one's calling in the life of faith
6. In spiritual direction there is attention to the influences of one's past and shadow through discernment and life review
7. In spiritual direction there is an orientation to the future life of faith and growth in grace
8. In spiritual direction the engagement in dialogue includes confrontation and clarification that foster cognitive and

Seeking the Holy

    affective dissonance—doubt, fear, recognition of one's shadow—are all brought in the open for discussion
9. In spiritual direction the context of the work is not just cognitive, but rather affective and spiritual
10. In spiritual direction spiritual growth is seen as taking place in the context of a faith community
11. In spiritual direction the emphasis is not on crisis resolution, but on continued, on-going spiritual growth
12. In spiritual direction the relationship is between two healthy, mutually supportive individuals in the context of love and friendship.

In the next chapter, we will review specific implications from the practice of direction for the spiritual formation education of persons in the contemporary congregation and faith community.

Chapter 5

Spiritual Direction and the Congregational Context

There currently is a strong desire in congregations to move away from the traditional educational models to formation models for Christian education. The best some congregations have been able to do is change the name of their educational programming from "Christian Education" to some variant that uses the term "formation." Regrettably, these efforts have been little more than a hopeful gesture that has kept old wine in old wineskins. Truthfully, congregations continue to suffer from a lack of effective discipleship due to a lack of understanding of both education and of formation. Certainly, this is tragic. Efforts at meeting the spiritual needs of the members of the church, from children to adults, are at best, benign, and at worst, inimical to growth in the faith. This chapter will explore the ways the ancient practice of spiritual direction can help re-shape formal Christian education formation programming in a community of faith—a church.

Spiritual direction is the practice and process that helps believes address the needs and spiritual dimensions in the journey of seeking the Holy. The practice of spiritual direction relies on foundational elements needed for spiritual formation: a spiritual epistemology, companionship, mentoring, attention to symbols, and methodologies that rely on spiritual disciplines and practices. Implicit in developmental psychologies is the concept that the second half of life is the time of greatest potential for spiritual maturity. Midlife is the point when the spiritual journey begins in earnest. Midlife marks the beginning of the second half of life in which there are emergent possibilities for unique psychological, emotional, and spiritual religious growth (or stagnation depending, to a great extent, on internal and external factors). Furthermore, psychologists like Jung have claimed that the root challenges in the second half of life are fundamentally inner spiritual crisis.

Reframing Christian Education Formation

Before exploring specific elements necessary in an adult religious education for the fostering of spiritual development, let us examine certain foundations need to make a transition toward a formation approach to Christian education. These foundational assumptions are informed by the practice of spiritual direction and the field of developmental psychologies. One foundational assumption grows out of the significant fact that became evident in the historical survey of spiritual direction, being that the truly innovative spiritual guides after the apostolic period were not pastors, as such, but educators and teachers.[191] This highlights the foundational assumption that spiritual development falls within the scope of discipleship education in the congregation, and is the main responsibility of religious education formation efforts of pastors, church staff and laypersons.

A second significant foundational assumption is that some form of spiritual guidance can be the overarching integrative factor in adult religious education—especially for those in mid-life. This assumption grows out of the fact that spiritual direction is ideally suited to the spiritual development of adults in the second half of life.[192] Through its orientation, goals and methods, direction helps meet the deep spiritual needs of the middlescent adult. Spiritual direction is unstructured and varied enough in form and methodology to attend to the specific needs of particular individuals within the church.[193] Religious educators who are doing an effective Christian education formation ministry likely are already engaged in spiritual direction of one form or another.

> Real spiritual companionship is one element in an adequate Christian education, and real religious education will initiate a process of religious experience and knowledge that will make use of sacraments, pastoral care and spiritual direction of whichever type the individuals require. Christian education has to be individually oriented if it is to be Christian.[194]

A third foundational assumption is that the kind of spiritual direction that is needed, especially in the context of Protestant religious education, is not a direct adoption of classic monastic direction or as presented in the spiritual classics. Fairchild pointed out that even contemporary Roman Catholics have rejected and drastically modified almost all of the assumptions of authoritarianism and clergy-laity distinctions found in classic spiritual direction.[195] Any legitimate application of spiritual direction in a contemporary local church setting will take into account modem psychologies, methodologies, research in religious education, and appropriate theological as well as pedagogical frameworks.

The Nature of Adult Religious Education for Formation

Surveys of developmental psychology and spiritual direction offer implications for fundamental assumptions concerning the nature of adult religious education for spiritual growth. For example, Erikson's and Jung's position that all data of human experience can be given a religious interpretation has implication for a broader, fuller understanding of the dimensions of the adult's religious experience.[196] This understanding broadens the scope of adult religious education. An adult religious education that is too narrowly defined in scope holds the danger of involving persons in only ecclesiastical concerns. "True religion must be concerned with the totality of human experience."[197]

Adult religious education must be presented as part of the adult's personal search for meaning and as part of the adult's religious experience. Adult religious education must help clarify for adults their religious and spiritual needs and dimensions. According to Elias: these needs include: . . . love, belonging, trust, acceptance, identity, freedom, positive self-concept, relations to others, understanding, relationship with the divine, and a sense of stability.[198] These needs should form the basis for any life-centered or experience-centered religious education. The inner realities and crises of development must be recognized and addressed by any adult religious education program that is to foster spiritual development.[199]

Lewis J. Sherrill provided a definition of religious education which is both broad enough and focused enough to serve as a comfortable description of the kind of adult religious education advocated in this study. Sherrill defined religious education as ". . . the attempt, ordinarily by members of the Christian community, to participate in and guide the changes which take place in persons in their relationships with God, with the church, with other persons, with the physical world, and with oneself."[200]

Epistemological Foundations

There are certain foundational epistemological assumptions needed in an education for spiritual growth. Some of these assumptions were found in Jung's psychology and in spiritual direction. Generally speaking, most adults, and their religious educators, are unaware of the structures which they use to organize and interpret their experiences. A major reason for this ignorance lies in a lack of a unified spiritual theology in the theological education of religious educators.[201] The gulf between academic theology and the practice of spiritual guidance has been a disastrous one. Educator Leon McKenzie observed that most adult religious educators receive academic training as conveyers of theological-biblical messages which they received from ". . . content specialists in the theological sciences."[202] Such an educational approach produces religious educators more concerned and comfortable with the message-content to be conveyed, and insufficiently concerned or knowledgeable about the learner and the processes of learning and spiritual development. The idea that a primary function of clergy and lay experts should be to guide people in their explorations of this spiritual domain is, from evidence, not considered a central task of the Church. Additionally, very few seminaries give any significant instruction or training in this area.[203]

Kelsey likened religious educators with little or no understanding of the process of spiritual growth to the blind leading the blind.[204] A knowledge of the tradition of spirituality is a critical element in the development of a desire for spiritual growth in adults and in adult religious educators.[205] The epistemological framework of most contemporary religious educators in this society is based mostly on a rationalistic materialism and objectivism.[206] Such an epistemological viewpoint tends to lead to a denial that there is a spiritual realm that can be known through experience—indeed, that a spiritual realm really exists at all. The epistemology of a religious education oriented to spiritual development is of a different nature. In this view the person accepts that both the physical world and the spiritual world are real. This is significant, for as Jung and Kelsey pointed out, "Human beings need to participate in both these worlds if they are to be fully alive."[207] In a religious education with an appropriate spiritually oriented epistemology, it is acknowledged that, ". . . none of us knows enough to assume that we human beings are confined only to sensory experience and a physical world: the individual's spiritual experiences, his prayer life, his religious intuitions should be examined and sifted and used as carefully as one's sensory experiences."[208] An understanding of a separate reality is basic to the spiritual exercises of Ignatius. Exercises and methods, however, are not sufficient in a religious education for spiritual development; they must grow out of an adequate and appropriate epistemological framework.[209] In this context Hinson warned—especially Protestant churches—that one ". . . must be careful not to restrict God's power in entering into human life and effecting change."[210] The practice of spiritual makes clear that the work of the Holy Spirit is necessary to any development in the religious life. This is true for an adult religious education in a congregation that strives for the spiritual development of its members.[211]

Both reviews of developmental psychologies and spiritual direction revealed another dimension symptomatic of an inadequate epistemological viewpoint in Christian education. Palmer called it an ". . . illness in our culture; it arises from our rigid separation of the visible world from the powers that undergird and animate it."[212] The polarization that results is a dichotomy of the secular and sacred. Edwards maintained that such a dichotomy leads to conditions within the church which includes a polarization of spirituality into intellectual and affective.[213] Palmer maintained that such a secular-sacred dichotomy results in a diminished life, capping off its sources of healing, hope, and wholeness.[214] In Jung's view this was the basic reason for the plight of modern persons. But as Tillich asserted, "Religion is not a special function of the human spirit."[215] This secular-sacred dichotomy results in an epistemological assumption that the various aspects of human development, and of the human experience, are isolated one from another.

When the interpretation of reality is segmented so is the perception of the individual adult segmented into realms of secular and profane. The result is a form of religious education in which there is a failure to take into account the total person, one which attempts to address only so-called sacred "parts" of the individual. One of the most Substantial flaws of most adult religious education, according to McKenzie, is the flaw of constricted focus. Subsequently, "educational activities exclusively revolve around topics that are religious in the most obvious sense."[216]

As a result of the bifurcation of the sacred from the spiritual and the intellect from the affect, subject areas that are able to serve the everyday needs and interests of adults in mid-life are totally disregarded. The implication for an adult religious education for spiritual development is that since spirituality (religion) permeates life, adult religious education needs to embrace all topics relevant to the adult's life, even those usually considered secular. In the final analysis, what makes religious education religious is determined by: 1) the content; 2) the intentionality of the teacher; 3) the intentionality of the learner; and 4) the psychological and cultural context of the learning experience.[217]

Most congregational Christian education programs continue to mimic instructional and academic approaches. They follow "schooling" models with didactic pedagogies and focus on acquiring knowledge and learning theological concepts. But O'Brien challenges this entrenched model by stating that "seldom do adults feel any need for a new ecclesiology of Christology. The challenge they face is to integrate smoothly their faith and their vocational interests."[218] In the review of the developmental psychologies, one important need of the adult during the second half of life is for a unified philosophy of life, or spiritual life structure. A religious education with a sacred-secular epistemological dichotomy does not help in meeting this need. Neither is one that over-focuses on the cognitive to the neglect of the affective. A religious education for spiritual development must provide a unified epistemology which helps the adult cultivate a unified spiritual life structure—belief and devotion, knowledge and compassion, understanding and obedience.

A formation approach to adult religious education for spiritual development, therefore, will attend to religious experience more so than on propositional truths, data, or methodology.[219] This is an assumption which clearly is found in the practice of spiritual direction. In this type of religious education, the educator tries to match the experience of the adult learner with the religious truths to be discovered and presented. Further, a religious education for spiritual development will actively engage in helping adults in opening doors to the experience of God and of the presence of the Holy. In this type of religious education, the process is as important, if not more important, than the content.

Congregations must provide the context and processes that will result in the opportunities to experience the interplay of relationships open to God. "The inestimable worth of religious experiences as a necessary focal point and key attribute of substantive content lies in the fact that living faith is not just a thought or a concept or a feeling. Rather, the practice of faith . . . is essentially a holistic experience in which the person existentially encounters in some way the actuality of God. . . ."[220]

Certainly, there is potential danger in a religious education that is solely experience based, but neither spiritual direction, nor the kind of religious education formation approach advocated here is so one—dimensional. Kelsey provided a concise definition which contains a key factor: "Real religious education should be an attempt . . . to guide each of us to an experience of God through loving concern guided by a knowledge of a religious tradition and sifted through critical understanding and knowledge of the religious experiences of others."[221] The critical factor by which both the content and the process of educational spiritual experiences in the church are to be evaluated is the Christian revelation itself. The word of God provides a compass that keeps the conversion journey of the individual on course as the spiritual learning experiences continue.[222]

In the type of religious education informed by the orientation of spiritual direction the adult is enabled to come to trust and value personal religious experiences and to integrate what is learned with awareness of the total meaning of life—the spiritual life structure.[223] All this grows out of a foundational assumption that an adult religious education for spiritual development has as its goal the personal integration of the individual.[224] One final and significant foundational assumption for the type of religious education for spiritual development is that an adult religious education for spiritual development will be more effective (and valid) if religious principles were used in teaching Christianity.[225] The methods as well as the content of a religious education for spiritual development need to grow out of the basic Christian assumptions of the nature of the person and his or her relation to God and others. Christianity's foundational and epistemological assumptions, intrinsically, are relational.

An Adult Religious Education Approach for Spiritual Formation

Having established some foundational assumptions concerning the adult religious education advocated in this study, attention is now turned to direct implications for a religious education for the spiritual development of the adult in mid-life. We will give our attention to the processes involved in an education whose prime concern to the adult in mid-life. Implications in two representative methodologies will be examined. The context of these implications primarily applies to religious education in the local church setting.

The Affective-Cognitive Dichotomy

The problem of an affective-cognitive dichotomy is of central concern in the matter of mid-life spiritual development. In the review of developmental psychologies it became clear that one of the central dynamics of mid-life development is the movement towards interiority in the adult with its subsequent discovery of a more affective, 'feminine' side of the self (especially for men). In spiritual direction attention is given to the awareness and fostering of the affective side of the adult. What became all too clear from psychologists and is the long history of spiritual direction is that a cognitive emphasis to spirituality and faith is totally inadequate for adult spiritual development.[226]

A highly developed affective consciousness is essential to the spiritual life. Epistemologically, this means that " . . . the intuitive way of knowing is fundamental to spirituality."[227] McKenzie pointed out that even the religious commitments of many adults are rooted not in rational analysis of theological propositions or biblical interpretations, but (as Jung maintained), in affective orientations toward religious symbols and ritual.[228] In an adult religious education for spiritual development, attention must be given to fostering affective spiritual autonomy, awareness, and development. Any religious education designed solely as a cognitive experience will not be of significant help in the development of the spiritual life of the adult.[229] The reason for this was made clear by Jung and has been succinctly echoed by Kelsey:

> Where rational consciousness deals in concepts and ideas, our inner lives and emotions, or affects, are generally presented to our *conscious* minds directly in images. Thus rational, cognitive thought, thinking which is just in the head, brings only a part of the human mind into play.[230]

The practical implication is clear: the adult teacher who uses only rational, cognitive tools does not reach the adult student as well as the educator who uses affect and images.[231]

Paradoxically, however, the necessity for a rational dimension to faith must also be addressed in religious education. Without reason, spirituality erodes into mere sentimentality. As mentioned above, there is needed a rational testing of subjective knowledge and religious experiences. (The spiritual exercises of Ignatius are excellent examples of this dynamic in action. Meditative techniques (e.g. active imagination) are carefully designed to avoid extremes of intellectualization or of floundering about is purely emotional experience).

The review of the practice of spiritual direction provided three areas where an adult religious education for spiritual development can help the adult in mid—life: the development of discernment: contemplation, and prayer. Education in these three areas can provide the adult learner with the opportunities to tap into the more affective and intuitional dimensions of self so necessary for spiritual development (and in this way overcoming the affective—cognitive dichotomy that inhibits spiritual development).

Discernment and contemplation in the second half of life critical to a sensitivity to the working of the Holy Spirit in the life of the person. Adults in the second half of life need to be aware of the meaning of daily experiences in work, home, and within the self in the context of a spiritual life structure.[232] Religious education in the spiritual formation approach can help adults learn how to reflect upon and integrate daily experiences and crises of self, meaning, death, and limitations, into their being. This awareness, reflection, and integration becomes possible when an ". . . openness exists for continuous, insightful learning."[233]

The religious life experiences of adults provide the context and content of their spiritual journeys. But without the ability to recognize and reflect upon the meaning and processes of this inner dimension, there is likely to result feelings of powerlessness, depression, and ". . . a bitterness directed to the closest external institution: profession, parenthood, church. This can profoundly disrupt the growth in faith during these formative adult years."[234] Every adult needs to be so educated in how to reflect upon (contemplate) his or her spiritual life structure and experiences in relation to self, God, and others.[235]

Another area that spiritual direction can contribute to an adult religious education formation approach in the congregation for spiritual growth is prayer. The implication is clear: religious education needs to provide adults in the second half of life resources for a life of prayer. The kind of prayer that needs to be fostered in these learning experiences is contemplative prayer, a prayer which is a response to God and to what God has done, and is doing, in the life of the believer. Prayer of this kind is one in which the adult listens for the works and words of God, and is based on an appropriate spiritual epistemology, ". . . one which recaptures and makes new the thought and prayer patterns of Jesus and his more Eastern, Hebraic companions."[236]

Contemplative prayer includes fostering the skill and capacity for discernment, the ability to make religious sense out of what adults experience in the living of their lives of faith.[237] This aspect of religious education formation includes providing adults with exercises, techniques and means aimed at helping them live in a fuller relationship with God. For example,

> . . . the examination of consciousness, meditation and contemplation techniques, the Way of the Cross, discernment exercises, and various means for praying . . . are only a few of the aids which need to be taught to

persons so that they can discover meaningful ways to enhance and enliven their relationships with God.[238]

Spiritual Generativity

Both developmental psychology and spiritual direction made clear that mature personal and spiritual development involves a movement inward (interiority and the ability for self-reflection and self-knowledge) and then a movement outward.[239] A religious education for spiritual development must provide for and foster a spiritual generativity. In a religious education formation approach imparting the faith requires opportunities for appropriate action in actual service to others on the part of the adult.[240]

A religious education for spiritual development must provide for middlescents involvement in a broad range of concerns and problems outside of themselves, as egocentrism, egoism, and egotism remain constant obstacles to spiritual growth well into adulthood. Moving outside of oneself, investing in the lives of others and in the generations to come are the only ways in which care and generativity can come to fruition. The crises of the second half of life (limitations, death, meaning, loss, generativity) should recast the focus of the adult religious education formation programs in the church. The reason many adult religious education programs fail in fostering spiritual development is that there is no provision, in a concrete way, for cultivating the generative person. An effective adult religious education for spiritual development will guide the adult learner through the movement inward, then toward a movement outward into personal involvement in the lives of others and in society.[241]

Community and Mentoring

The reviews of developmental psychologies and of spiritual direction revealed the need for community and mentoring (or sponsorship) in the life of the adult. The spiritual life has a definite communal dimension to it that cannot be ignored.[242] An adult religious education for spiritual development will provide the environment for the fostering of a community that actively engages in sponsorship and encourages the development of all the dimensions of the spiritual self.

An important task of the faith community is to provide role models for the spiritual life. The religious community needs to be able to recognize and call forth those within itself who have reached the maturity that will enable them to be mentors and stewards of the faith.[243] To be Christian means to be part of a community and to take responsibility and accountability in the community relationship seriously.[244] Religious educator Charles R. Foster insisted that the ministry of teaching belongs to the whole community, saying that "The community is ultimately responsible to introducing people into its life."[245] This is part of the biblical idea of covenant, which will require of adults to take time to regularly review and evaluate their lives, and be helped to be more faithful. "Such activity in the life of the church is essential to providing role models for the spiritual life."[246]

This necessitates, of course, that a good number of persons in the community, who are in the second half of life, have achieved a certain level of adult spiritual development and have become able to share their faith journey with each other. Some of the finest spiritual guides for adults in the second half of life can be found among the lay persons within the community.[247] For an effective formation education program in a congregation, the understanding of spirituality needs to be defined in adult terms and language appropriate to adult development. For example,

> . . . an individual who is working through to social responsibility cannot be helped by a community which sponsors a dichotomization between religious and social realities, or which preaches humility and spiritual childhood to a person who is experiencing and coping to terms with an authentic sense of creative power. The community's task is not to distract or shelter adults in mid-life from the crises in their lives. Rather, there is the attempt to assist adults in confronting those challenges so that ". . . within the psychological stress of this time, God's unanticipated but inviting presence can be discerned."[248]

Religious educators need to foster a climate of freedom in the community of faith. In this climate, adults will feel free and at ease in searching for authentic selfhood within the framework of the community's people and tradition. "Such a climate will become productive as persons learn to deal openly and honestly with the vital issues of faith and the real questions of their own lives."[249]

The openness and acceptance fostered in such a community helps curtail the dangers of reliance solely on subjective religious experience while legitimizing the necessary attention to the affective dimension in an adult religious education for spiritual development. In a faith community, interpretations of the individual's religious experiences are provided in the context of the community tradition of Scriptural interpretation. Insights and experiences are not isolated within individuals, but shared, and members are helped to discover the meaning of experience in the context of shared community and tradition. Palmer shared the significance of the community in this respect on a personal level:

> In the gathered life of the spiritual community, I am brought out of solitude of study and prayer into the discipline of communion and relatedness. The community is a check against my personal distortions; it helps interpret the meaning of texts and gives guidance in my experience of prayer. But life in community is also a continual testing and refining of the fruits of love in my life. Here, in relation to others, I can live out (or discover I am lacking) the peace and joy, the humility and servanthood by which spiritual growth is measured.[250]

Teaching as Relationship

Teaching is primarily a relational activity. Likewise, the dimension of spiritual direction that contributes to its effectiveness in fostering spiritual development is its relational process. An adult religious education for spiritual development must refocus its foundational understanding of teaching from its being a technique, method, activity, or art, to teaching as a relationship.

Seeking the Holy

Henri J. M. Nouwen correctly argued that religious education is not primarily ministry because of the content, but because of the nature of the education process itself. He warned that "Perhaps we have paid too much attention to the content of teaching without realizing that the teaching relationship is the most important factor in the ministry of teaching."[251]

In an adult religious education for spiritual development, the most meaningful interaction and the greatest potential for learning and growth takes place between person and person in the context of a community of faith.[252] And the most effective condition for communication of faith is, as was evident from both psychologists and spiritual directors, love between teacher and learner. The teaching relationship is a clear example where the foundational assumption that religious education must use Christian principles if it is to be effective, must be put into practice.

Teaching as relationship has radical implications for the teacher in an adult religious education for spiritual development. First, in this kind of teaching, content and a focus on cognitive learning are secondary. The teacher can only communicate as much Christianity as he or she has assimilated and is living, and that goes beyond merely knowing more.[253] Being a teacher for the spiritual development of adults in the second half of life involves ". . . paying the price of letting God work you over, being purified by the fire of divine love, undergoing transformation from within by divine grace."[254] Second, since relationship is the most important dynamic in an adult religious education for spiritual development, and accepting the assumption of spiritual direction that the Holy Spirit is the real source of spiritual direction and growth, then any number of members of the community can be called upon to be a spiritual director/ educator. In most churches, more members than we suspect can be the kind of companion (spiritual friend) to others who can facilitate spiritual growth.

An adult religious education for spiritual development will call adults in the second half of life to be that sort of spiritual companion in their communities of faith. Religious educators need to work at giving adults confidence, training, and opportunities for such faith relationships. Too often, traditional schooling models of Christian education serve mainly to keep people dependent perpetual "pupils" to a select group of teachers-as-experts. But fostering spiritual development is not the exclusive responsibility or calling of clergy.[255] As Jones said, "we often underestimate the spiritual resources and capacities of human beings and thereby deny the power and grace of God working and struggling in us."[256]

Third, teaching as relationship involves, paradoxically, both submission and mutuality. Progress in the spiritual life is enhanced when persons make themselves accountable to another, be it an individual or community. Without submission, the learner cannot learn or benefit from the discernments, teachings, or direction of another—teacher, mentor, or spiritual companion. At the same time, teaching as relationship involves a genuine mutuality between teacher and learner. This mutuality was found even among the Desert Fathers.[257] Again, neither clergy, teachers, educators, nor mentors have a monopoly on spiritual growth, nor on the capacity to participate in that ministry in a faith community.

Fourth, teaching as relationship involves an operational acceptance of the foundational assumption of relationship as I-Thou. Neither teacher nor student, director or directee, is an object to the other—both are subjects in relationship one with another and both with God.

Fifth, teaching as relationship means that the lives of the adults—their experience of the life of faith—will be the main "educational content" of the learning experience. Dialogue in an adult religious education for spiritual development revolves around finding meaning in the spiritual life structure and experiences of adults themselves.[258]

Sixth, teaching as relationship implies that the adult teacher, leader, or guide will be open and subject to change, and being changed, themselves. Taking the fundamental assumptions of the kind of adult religious education for spiritual development advocated here, it can be no other way. There can be no 'safety' in the role of teacher, because teaching involves mutuality, submission, dependency and accountability in the relationship of the teacher with pupil and community.

Implications for Methodological Approaches

An effective and adult religious education for spiritual development must take seriously the foundational assumption that

Christians need to be educated according to Christian principles if spiritual development is to take place. "The medium of the communication must be consonant with the message, or the message will be garbled or not taken seriously."[259] A major goal of a religious education for spiritual development is to help the adult live in a responsive relationship with God, self and others. The methodology used in such an education must be consonant with that goal. Methodology must help provide the environment in which channels of communication and dialogue between the teacher, the adult learner, and God, are opened. "The message is heard and received in proportion to the degree that the climate encourages spirit-filled receptiveness, the sharing of insights, and personal growth."[260]

Symbols, Stories, and Myths

Let's examine more closely two areas of methodology for spiritual growth: 1) the use of symbols, stories, and myths; and 2) the use of small groups. In the reviews of developmental psychologies and of spiritual direction, the significance of symbols are central for growth, integration, and formation. Jung, for example, maintained that myth, symbol, and ritual have always been the language religion, a sentiment echoed by Fowler. An adult religious education for spiritual development must recognize the fact that symbolic language is a necessary element in its methodology. Religious educators need to exploit the treasure house of religious symbolism at their disposal and to set about recovering its meaning for adults today. The language of adult religious education must be a language that helps the adult relate ". . . to the infinite, to the ultimate, to God."[261]

As Jung and Fowler demonstrated, the content of a symbol cannot be fully grasped or expressed in rational terms. Significant to the adult in mid-life, the process of individuation is expressed in ". . . symbols of an irrational nature."[262] Jung called symbols the transcendent function which helps in the process of individuation—the union of opposites and the healing of the divided self. In terms of spiritual development,

> . . . in experiencing the profound symbolic contents of his psyche, the believer will encounter the eternal principles which confirm the workings of God within him and reinforce his belief that God created man in his own image.[263]

Those methods which help adults in mid—life make connections between symbols and the experiences in their lives are the most effective in an adult religious education for spiritual development.

A number of educators have become sensitive to the significance of symbol in the spiritual development of adults. Recently, the Jungian approach to dreams as personal reflections and manifestations of the collective unconscious has been given greater attention.[264] According to Jung, the dream was the easiest and most effective way of investigating the mechanisms and contents of the unconscious, which is necessary to the process of individuation.[265] Though the dream is rarely addressed in most adult religious education programs, it remains a significant element, as was recognized by Christian educator Cully. "Encouraging people to become aware of and sensitive to symbols and their meanings and to apprehend dreams, along with the potential spiritual dimensions of dreaming, are areas through which education in the spiritual life can be enriched."[266]

A less mystic method which will help the adult in the journey of the second half of life capture the meaning of symbol is the use of personal life stories, or, myths. Personal life stories, as identified by psychologists like Jung, Fowler, and Vaillant, and as utilized in spiritual direction, help adults get in touch with meaning in their lives. Personal stories that help adults understand who they are must include some explanation of the meaning of human existence in the cosmos and express one's encounter with reality.[267] For Jung, stories and myths spring from one's experience of psychic wholeness, that is, as a result of the integration of conscious and unconscious.

> Living a story, whether it be the 'old, old story' of Christian hymnody that grasps us, or some new image of truth that reveals itself to us, is the way we experience meaning and value in our lives. Living a story (finding, as Jung says, 'our myth') is what provides us with a framework for choosing the values we will serve.[268]

Stories are essential for describing the Christian experience. Stories were masterfully used by Jesus to describe what a person's relationship to God should be like. Customarily, Jesus used vivid imagery drawn from the everyday life of his listeners (their life structures). Until the time of the printed text, and the Reformation shortly after, images (e.g. stained glass windows, icons, art) and storytelling were the main means of communicating the Gospels.

Adults in the second half of life need to Learn how to tell their own personal faith story. The ability to tell one's own personal story helps in recovering a sense of wholeness. Sharing one's story helps in recovering an appreciation for experiences of mystery and moments of communion with the Holy.[269] An adult religious education for spiritual development will aid middlescents (through meditation and discernment) to reflect on the grace-filled fragments of the narrative of their lives and to make connections with the divine story. They may then discern ". . . where God has been luring and leading."[270] Fairchild suggested that for Protestants, the sharing of one's personal life story should be the central paradigm of spiritual guidance.[271]

Small Groups

Another methodological implication for an education for spiritual *development* grows out of a combination of the identified dynamics discussed above. First, it was established that the most effective teaching methods for spiritual development are relational ones: those that are experiential, personal, and interactive. Second, it was established that spiritual development (and direction) takes place in the context of a community; one cannot go it alone on the spiritual journey. In the *I—Ching* is stated; "The superior man joins with his friends for discussion and practice. . . . There is always something ponderous and one-sided about the learning of the self—taught."[272] Out of these two established dynamics in the process of an education for spiritual development grows the final implication to be drawn in this study: an adult religious education for spiritual development needs to provide and use small groups as a primary methodology.

According to Edwards, group spiritual guidance is the standard form of guidance in Christian tradition.[273] Of significance is Roy H. Ryan's contention that the small group approach is in keeping theologically with the nature of the church as a community of faith.[274] Such an assertion supports the importance of the principle that an effective religious education must use Christian principles.

The sharing of spiritual life stories consistently works best in small groups (fifteen or less) where there is an intentional process of interaction among members. This dialogical process becomes the primary method for the group learning dynamic.[275] The committed use of small groups of adults for fostering spiritual development holds the greatest potential for revitalizing the adult religious education of the church in helping adults on their spiritual journey. Any religious or spiritual content can efficiently be taught in a small group using dialogical methods. After this, the most important dimensions of the small group method—that of engaging adult learners in the learning and relational processes—can be utilized to the greatest advantage. The goal of the mall group must be the same as that of spiritual direction: to aid adults in hearing and responding to God and others in the context of relationship.

A number of processes that are possible only in small groups can be used to help foster spiritual formation and development in adults. First, a small group can provide the intimate and supportive environment in which adults can feel free to meaningfully share their spiritual life story. Second, in a small group, adults receive the opportunity to discover their own reactions to the insights and wisdom shared and can reflect on their significance to what is happening in their own lives.

Third, "In this situation, most people will discover the value of allowing images to rise in prayer, and thus they find a new sense of conviction about the reality of God and the elements of spirit that make up this kingdom."[276] Fourth, a small group can become the mediating and interpreting community for the personal religious experiences of the individual group member. Clift contended that perhaps the basic challenge to Christianity posed by Jung's observations about the group experience is that the reality of God and of one's inner experience of God must never be lost in one's experience of groups and community.[277] Fifth, as the most immediate and intimate expression of the adult's religious community, the small group can provide the imagery for the individual's world view. Sixth, the small group is capable of combining all other forms of group spiritual guidance as appropriate, together with a limited amount of one-to-one direction. Seventh, small groups can fill the gap left by the shortage of available, experienced, and qualified one-on-one spiritual directors.

While the efficacious dynamics of the small group method are fundamental, the methodological variety is almost limitless. One such variety that has been used in spiritual direction and for spiritual development is the spiritual retreat. The spiritual retreat is designed to help persons develop a new perspective and fresh vision of their spiritual life structure. This is done by offering adults opportunities to distance themselves from their immediate life situations. Unfortunately for most Protestants a "retreat" ". . . is frequently only a synonym for conference, for which a program is carefully planned, speakers are selected, discussions arranged, and worship services structured."[278] Little opportunity is given to participants for those processes found in spiritual direction: silence, reflection, introspection, listening to the word of God (or merely waiting on God), or spending time in meaningful spiritual dialogue with a spiritual friend. Much can be learned from silent retreats and programs like that found in Ignatius' *Spiritual Exercises*, that can be of great value in a religious education for adults in mid-life.

Spiritual direction in a religious education setting can be offered to adults through small groups that have as their explicit goal the spiritual development of its members. Hinson suggested that the "Voluntary formation of groups for Bible study, discussion of Christian classics, meditation, or personal growth may be the best way to augment incentives built into the routine church program"[279] most members experience and come to expect of their church's educational opportunities. In the context of adult religious education in a congregation, it cannot be overstated that participation in small groups for spiritual development needs to be completely voluntary.

Evelyn and James Whitehead provided a statement that serves as an excellent summary of the significance of the small group for the adult in mid-life.

> Growth groups with capable leaders . . . can provide the caring and protective atmosphere in which an adult attempts to reconcile her dream and to balance anew the polarities and ambiguities within the self. Programs of leadership development can assist maturing Christians to focus their generative energies more broadly in activities of social concern and ministry. Such explicit attention to the details and dynamics of these transitions can support adults in identifying and responding to the graces, limitations, and failures that have shaped their lives. In such heightened awareness the processes of forgiveness, healing, and reorientation can begin.[280]

Limitations and Challenges

One of the most crucial issues confronting adult religious education in congregations today is the issue of helping their members achieve spiritual maturity. According to religious educator Leon McKenzie, "If we are not concerned about spiritual development, it serves no good for us to be concerned about anything else."[281] Though spiritual direction and developmental psychology hold great promise in aiding an adult religious education for spiritual growth in contemporary congregations, there are certain limitations and challenges that must be addressed. Many of these have been alluded to previously in this study and so at this point, only mention is made of them. For brevity's sake, these limitations and cautions are delineated briefly:

1. Although developmental psychology provides great insight into personal development and the dynamics of personal growth, it has limitations in the realm of the spiritual dimensions of religious experience.

2. Until conscientious consideration is given to key foundational assumptions concerning spiritual development and adult religious education, very likely there will be incongruity between intent and methodology in how congregations engage in programs and activities carried out under the name "formation."

3. The kind of religious education formation for spiritual development advocated in this study will not be of benefit to all adults, only to those who are mature, psychologically and emotionally healthy, and well along in their personal spiritual development.

4. In terms of spiritual leadership in the local church, it is unlikely that every pastor will or even can become a spiritual guide. Nor will it be that those persons charged with oversight of educational programs understand educational process, formation, or the principles of spiritual direction sufficient to inform programs and educational experiences.

5. The creation of the kind of adult religious education advocated in this study will take a long time and will face great resistance in most local churches.

6. In Protestant churches there may tend to be a paucity of tradition which contains the richness of imagery needed for the effective use of some aspects of spiritual direction—both group and individual.

7. The danger exists that attempts at spiritual direction in a local church may become packaged, standardized programs so as to again ". . . muffle the inner voice rather than to promote those conditions of personal freedom in which it can be truly heard."[282]

8. In a local church setting, there is the danger that individual spiritual direction may be stressed at the expense of community formation and nurture in correctives are not provided for the individualistic culture in which most churches and their members live.

9. Inherent in the process of spiritual direction are the dangers of manipulation, transference, exploitation, and a perpetuation of mutual spiritual shallowness and prejudices. This reality makes the importance of having trained and certified directors as resources to congregations and their educational leaders.

10. Spiritual guidance in group or individual direction will work only if it is voluntary and sought by the person receiving it. The journey of seeking the Holy cannot be coerced.

11. Group spiritual direction is subject to all the limitations and dangers inherent in group dynamics (manipulation, loss of goal, deterioration of purpose, pooling of ignorance, power struggles within the group and with the community at large, cliques, etc.).

12. The salient Eucharistic element of spiritual direction as found in the Catholic tradition will not likely have a place (or equivalent) in Protestant spiritual direction in the context of congregational religious and theological traditions.

One final dimension of an adult religious education for spiritual development needs to be addressed, for it has great relevance to the local church. Few more important tasks exist today in the area of religious education than that of equipping men and women as spiritual guides to adults. In terms of the kind of religious education presented in this study, if there is any place where education should follow these principles it is in the training of men and women preparing for the Christian ministry. Tragically, Kelsey contended that "If there is any place where this educational knowledge is almost totally ignored or unknown it is within the seminaries of our churches."[283] Westerhoff maintained that educational leaders in the seminaries do know better, but that,

> nevertheless, we continue to educate and graduate theological students who are bright but not wise, who know how to make a living as professional ministers, but who do not always know how to live as a spiritual resource for others. Today we ordain clergy who probably are better educated, in terms of knowledge and skills, than ever

before, but who may not be more holy or whole. Unless our identity is hid in God, we will never be able to fulfill our calling as spiritual guides, for a spiritual guide is one who prays, that is, one who meditates in solitude and silence in the love of God and the activity of God so that in a mysterious way she or he is enabled and empowered to nurture others in their relationship with God.[284]

Most seminarians, having not yet reached forty, have not attained the level of spiritual development that will carry them through the second half of life.[285] A seminary that does not aid in the spiritual formation of its own seminarians does them a great disservice. Ways must be developed of doing spiritual direction in and through learning institutions to help them ". . . become self-renewing social systems in which individual wholeness will be nurtured, not negated."[286] Admittedly, in the last decade seminaries have increased their attention to spirituality and formation, though both academic courses and experiential formative practices of the seminary experience. However, many of the emphases on spirituality remain more academic than formative, and there are yet enough theological Faculties with sufficient expertise or experience in formation psychology, pedagogy, and practices to be of significant help as spiritual guides to seminarians. Until seminaries make conscious efforts to use religious principles in their adult religious education programs for their ministers local churches will be limited in terms of actualizing the kind of adult religious education for spiritual development examined in this study.

NOTES

[1] *New Catholic Encyclopedia*, 1967 ed., s.v. "Direction, Spiritual," by K. A. Wall.

[2] Katherine Marie Dyckman and L. Patrick Carroll, *Inviting the Mystic, Supporting the Prophet: An Introduction to Spiritual Direction* (New York: Paulist Press, 1981), p. 20.

[3] William A. Barry, "Spiritual Direction and Pastoral Counseling," *Pastoral Psychology* 26 (Fall 1977): 9.

[4] Sandra Marie Schneiders, *Spiritual Direction* (Chicago: National Sisters Vocation Conference, 1977), pp 18-19 as cited in Roy W. Fairchild, "The Pastor as Spiritual Director," *Quarterly* Review 5 (Summer 1985): 27.

[5] William A. Barry and William J. Connolly, *The Practice of Spiritual Direction* (Seabury Press, 1982), p. 8.

[6] Thurian is quoted in Kenneth Leech, *Soul Friend: The Practice of Christian Spirituality,* Introduction by Henri J. M.Nouwen (San Francisco: Harper & Row, 1977), p. 34.

[7] See Dyckman, *Inviting the Mystic*, p. 20; Raymond Studzinsky, *Spiritual Direction and Midlife Development*, (Chicago: Loyola University Press, 1985), p. 6; Leech, *Soul Friend: The Practice of Christian Spirituality*, p. 35.

[8] Studzinski, *Spiritual Direction and Midlife Development,* p. 6.

[9] Roy W. Fairchild, "The Pastor as Spiritual Director," p. 25.

[10] John H.Westherhoff III, "The Pastor as Spiritual Director," *Quarterly Review* (Summer 1985): 45.

[11] *New Catholic Encyclopedia,* 1967 ed., s.v. "Direction, Spiritual," by K. A. Wall.

[12] Tilden Edwards, *Spiritual Friend* (New York: Paulist Press, 1980), p. 39.

[13] Leech, *Soul Friend*, p. 41. See Israel Galindo, *Stories of the Desert Fathers* (Educational Consultants, 2015).

[14] E. Glenn Hinson, "Recovering the Pastor's Role as Spiritual Guide," in *Spiritual Dimensions of Pastoral Care*, ed. By F. C. Senn (New York: Paulist Press, 1986), p. 32.

[15] For an in-depth treatment of Gregory the Great and spiritual direction, see Thomas C. Oden, *Care of Souls in The Classic Tradition*, Theology and Pastoral Care Series (Philadelphia: Fortress Press, 1984), pp. 43-74. See also Leech, Soul Friend, pp. 42, 49-50.

[16] *New Catholic Encyclopedia,* s.v. "Direction, Spiritual."

[17] Hinson, "Recovering the Pastor's Role as Spiritual Guide," p. 33-34.

[18] Leech, *Soul Friend*, p. 51.

[19] Ibid.

[20] *New Catholic Encyclopedia,* s.v. "Direction, Spiritual."

[21] Ibid.

[22] See Hinson, "Spiritual Guide," p. 34; Leech, *Soul Friend,* pp. 53-54; *New Catholic Encyclopedia*, s.v. "Direction, Spiritual."

[23] Leech, *Soul Friend,* p. 54.

[24] Ibid.

[25] Ibid., pp. 54-55.

[26] Hinson, "Spiritual Guide," p. 14.

[27] Ibid.

[28] Ibid.

[29] Glenn Hinson, "Puritan Spirituality," in *Protestant Spiritual Traditions*, ed. Frank C. Senn (New York: Paulist Press, 1986), pp. 169-70.

[30] John Weborg, "Pietism: 'The Fire of God . . .Which Flames in the Heart of Germany'" in *Protestant Spiritual Traditions*, p. 200.

[31] Hinson, "Spiritual Guide," p. 36.

[32] John T. McNeill, *A History of the Cure of Souls* (New York: Harper & Brothers, 1951), p. 276.

[33] *New Catholic Encyclopedia*, s.v. "Direction, Spiritual."

[34] Hinson, "Spiritual Guide," p. 36. See *The Spiritual Exercises of St. Ignatius,* trans. Anthony Mottola, Intro by Robert W. Gleason (New York: Doubleday & Co., Image Books, 1964); For an account of Ignatius' own spiritual journey, see Ignatius of Loyola, *The Autobiography,* trans. Joseph F. O'Callaghan, ed. John C. Olin (New York: Harper & Row, 1974).

[35] Leech, *Soul Friend,* p. 61.

[36] *New Catholic Encyclopedia*, s.v. "Direction, Spiritual."

[37] Ibid.

[38] Leech, *Soul Friend*, pp. 65-67.

[39] McNeill, "The Cure of Souls," p. 293; Fairchild, "The Pastor as Spiritual Director," p. 28.

[40] *New Catholic Encyclopedia*, s.v. "Direction, Spiritual."

[41] Studzinski, *Spiritual Direction and Midlife Development* p. 124.

[42] *New Catholic Encyclopedia*, s.v. "Direction, Spiritual"; Leech, *Soul Friend,* p. 74.

[43] See Wallace B. Clift, *Jung and Christianity: The Challenge of Reconciliation* (New York: Crossroad, 1982), pp. 82-83.

[44] Hinson, "Spiritual Guide," p.36.

[45] Gerald May, *Care of Mind/Care of Spirit: Psychiatric Dimensions of Spiritual Direction* (San Francisco: Harper & Row, 1982), p. 2; See also McNeill, *Cure of Souls*, p. 272.

[46] May, *Care of Mind/Care of Spirit,* p. 4.

[47] Fairchild, "Spiritual Director," p. 28.

[48] Edwards, *Spiritual Friend,* p. 99.

[49] John Packard and Ashleigh Hope, *Church Refugees: Sociologists Reveal Why People Are DONE With Church But Not Their Faith* (Group: Loveland, CO, 2015).

[50] Edwards, p.100.

[51] Ibid., pp. 1-2.

[52] Barry and Connolly, *The Practice of Spiritual Direction*, p. 136.

[53] Jean Laplace, *Preparing for Spiritual Direction* trans. J. C. Guinnesss (Chicago: Franciscan Herald Press, 1975), p. 102.

[54] Hendrix is cited in Barry, "Spiritual Direction," p.4.

[55] Ibid.

[56] Dyckman, *Inviting the Mystic*, p. 48; Leech, *Soul Friend*, p. 111; Josef Sudbrack, *Spiritual Guidance* trans. Peter Heinegg (New York: Paulist Press, 1983), p. 32; Gratton, *Guidelines*, p. 110.

[57] Alan Jones, *Exploring Spiritual Direction: And Essay on Christian Friendship* (Minneapolis: Seabury Press, Winston Press, 1982), p. 37.

[58] Morton Kelsey, *Companions on the Inner Way: The Art of Spiritual Guidance* (New York: Crossroad, 1986), p. 42.

[59] Kelsey, *Companions*, pp. 41 and 59; Sudbrack, *Spiritual Guidance*, pp. 18-19.

[60] Studzinski, *Spiritual Direction*, p. 7.

[61] Jones, *Spiritual Direction*, p. 48.

[62] Leech, *Spiritual Friend*, p.28.

[63] Studzinski, *Spiritual Direction*, p. 7.

[64] Dyckman, *Inviting the Mystic,* p. 24.

[65] Gratton, *Guidelines,* pp. 61-64, 96; Leech, *Soul Friend,* p. 120.

[66] Tiffany Barnhouse, "Spiritual Direction and Psychotherapy," *Journal of Pastoral Care* 33 (1979): 152.

[67] Studzinski, *Spiritual Direction,* p. 9

[68] Gratton, *Guidelines*, pp. 83 and 85.

[69] Ibid., pp.83-90.

[70] Jones, *Spiritual Direction*, p.41.

[71] Edwards, *Spiritual Friend*, p. 29.

[72] Jones, *Spiritual Direction*, p. 20.

[73] Edwards, *Spiritual Friend*, p. 53.

[74] Ibid., p. 31.

[75] Gratton, *Guidelines*, p. 78.

[76] Barry and Connolly, *Spiritual Direction*, p.11.

[77] Studzinski, *Spiritual Direction*, p. 6.

[78] Ibid., p. 8.

[79] Edwards, *Spiritual Friend*, p. 98.

[80] Ibid., p. 99.

[81] Jones, *Spiritual Direction*, pp. 41, 47-48.

[82] Dyckman, *Inviting the Mystic*, pp. 24-25.

[83] Ibid., p. 27.

[84] Gratton, *Spiritual Direction*, p. 105.

[85] Gordon E. Jackson, *Pastoral Care and the Process of Theology* (Lanham, MD: University Press of America, Inc., 1981), p. 45.

[86] Damien Isabell, *The Spiritual Director: A Practical Guide* (Chicago: Franciscan Herald Press, 1976), p. 34.

[87] Dyckman, *Inviting the Mystic*, p. 7.

[88] Jones, *Spiritual Direction*, p.66.

[89] Gratton, *Guidelines*, p. 110.

[90] Barnhouse, "Spiritual Direction and Psychotherapy," pp. 152-153.

[91] Jones, *Spiritual Direction*, p. 64.

[92] Ibid., p. 64.

[93] Hinson, "Spiritual Guide," p. 37.

[94] Leech, "Spiritual Friend," p. 101

[95] Dyckman, *Inviting the Mystic,* p. 33; Gratton, *Guidelines,* pp. 80, 114; Barnhouse, "Spiritual Direction and Psychotherapy," p. 153.

[96] Fairchild, "Spiritual Director," p.31.

[97] Ibid.

[98] Jones, "Spiritual Direction," p. 56.

[99] Laplace, *Spiritual Direction*, p. 90; Jones, *Spiritual Direction,* p. 54

[100] See James Fowler, Stages of Faith: *The Psychology of Human Development and the Quest for Meaning.* San Francisco; Harper & Row, 1981.

[101] Studzinski, *Spiritual Direction*, p. 5.

[102] Barry and Connolly, *Spiritual Direction,* p. 17; Ibid., p.31.

[103] Studzinski, *Spiritual Direction,* p. 135; see John 14:25-26; Gratton, *Guidelines*, p. 95; Laplace, *Spiritual Direction*, p. 94.

[104] Jones, *Spiritual Direction*, p. 40; Isabell, *Spiritual Director*, p. 39.

[105] John of the Cross, *The Collected Works of John of the Cross*, trans. Kieren Kavanaugh, O.C.D. (Washington: ICS Publications, 1973), p.621 as cited in Jones, *Spiritual Direction*, p. 79.

[106] Studzinski, *Spiritual Direction*, p. 116.

[107] Gratton, *Guidelines*, p. 92.

[108] Francis W. Vanderwall, *Spiritual Direction: An Invitation to Abundant Life* (New York: Paulist Press, 1980), p. 4.

[109] Kelsey, *Companions*, p.90.

[110] Jones, *Spiritual Direction*, p. 32.

[111] Gratton, *Guidelines,* p. 90.

[112] Josef Sudbrack, *Spiritual Guidance*, trans. by Peter Heinegg (New York: Paulist Press, 1983), p. 43.

[113] Ibid. p. 55; c.f. Gerald G. May, "The Psychodynamics of Spirituality: A Follow-Up." *The Journal of Pastoral Care* 31 (June 1977): 90.

[114] Jones, *Spiritual Direction*, p. 32.

[115] Ibid., p. 54.

[116] Hinson, "Spiritual Guide," p.28.

[117] Kelsey, *Companions*, p. 90.

[118] -Ibid., p. 90.

[119] Gratton, *Guidelines*, p. 93.

[120] Vanderwall, *Spiritual Direction*, p. 12.

[121] Gratton, *Guidelines*, p. 97; Kelsey, *Companions*, p. 111; Jones, *Spiritual Direction*, p. 31.

[122] Dyckman, *Inviting the Mystic,* p. 25.

[123] Leech, *Soul Friend*, p.129.

[124] Barry and Connolly, *Spiritual Direction*, p. 102.

[125] Leech, *Soul Friend*, p. 77; Gratton, *Guidelines*, p.108; Studzinski, *Spiritual Direction*, p. 74.

[126] Studzinski, *Spiritual Direction*, p. 74.

[127] Sudbrack, *Spiritual Guidence*, p. 37.

[128] Ibid., pp.46, 56.

[129] See Conn's discussion on cognitive and affective conversion and self-knowing in adulthood in, "Conversion: A Developmental Perspective," *Cross Currents* 32 (1982): 332-33.

[130] Carl G. Jung, *Collected Works*, vol. 9, pt. 2: *Aion: Researchers into the Phenomenology of the Self*, p. 8.

[131] Loretta Girzaitis, "Adult Reflective Growth," *Religious Education* 72 (March-April 1977): 228.

[132] Jones, *Spiritual Direction*, p. 64.

[133] Laplace, *Spiritual Direction*, p. 27.

[134] Dyckman, *Inviting the Mystic*, p. 35.

[135] Gratton, *Guidelines*, p. 109.

[136] Leech, *Soul Friend*, pp.108-109; see also Laplace, *Spiritual Direction*, p. 39.

[137] Clift, *Jung and Christianity*, p. 43.

[138] Kelsey, *Companions*, p. 111.

[139] Studzinski, *Spiritual Direction*, p.6.

[140] Gratton, *Guidelines*, pp.106-107; see also Dyckman, *Inviting the Mystic*, p.27.

[141] Sudbrack, *Spiritual Guidance*, pp. 38-39.

[142] Henry C. Simmons, "Human Development: Some Conditions for Adult Faith at Age Thirty," *Religious Education* 71 (November-December 1976): 567; see also Sudbrack, Spiritual Guidance, p. 52.

[143] Evelyn E. and James D. Whitehead, *Christian Life Patterns: The Psychological Challenges and Religious Invitations of Adult Life* (Garden City, N.Y.: Doubleday and Co., 1979), p. 43.

[144] Barry and Connolly, *Spiritual Direction*, p. 8.

[145] Edwards, *Spiritual Friend*, p. 6.

[146] For a related study on this matter, see Bernard Lonergan, *Method in Theology* (New York: Herder & Herder, 1972), pp. 108ff. For Lonergan, theological

method is grounded on the religious experience of being in love with God, not on propositional deductions of content. See also Gordon Allport, *Becoming* (New Haven: Yale University Press, 1955).

[147] Studzinski, *Spiritual Direction*, p.5.

[148] Barry and Connolly, *Spiritual Direction*, pp. 110-111.

[149] Ibid., p. 110.

[150] Kelsey, *Companions*, p. 38; see also Morton Kelsey, *Discernment: A Study in Ecstasy and Evil* (New York: Paulist Press, 1978), pp. 82, 107ff; Barry and Connolly, *Spiritual Direction*, p.109.

[151] Barry and Connolly, *Spiritual Direction*, p. 148.

[152] Dyckman, *Inviting the Mystic*, p. 79.

[153] Whitehead and Whitehead, *Christian Life Patterns*, p.151; Donald Evans, *Struggle and Fulfillment: The Inner Dynamics of Religion and Morality* (Philadelphia: Fortress Press, 1979), p.148.

[154] Gratton, *Guidelines*, p. 87.

[155] Jones, *Spiritual Direction*, p. 24.

[156] Ignatius of Loyola, *The Spiritual Exercises*, p. 26.

[157] Barry and Connolly, *Spiritual Direction*, p. 57.

[158] Vanderwall, *Spiritual Direction*, p. 15.

[159] Studzinski, *Spiritual Direction*, pp. 83-84.

[160] Charles Stewart, "Mid-Life Crisis From a Faith Perspective," *Quarterly Review* 2 (Fall 1982): p. 71.

[161] Kelsey, *Companions*, p. 110; cf. Jones, *Spiritual Direction*, p. 38 and Jolande Jacobi, *The Psychology of C. G. Jung*, rev. ed. (New Haven: Yale University Press, 1962), p. 143.

[162] Martha Robbins, "The Desert-Mountain Experience: The Two Faces of Encounter With God," *The Journal of Pastoral Care* 35 (March 1981): 19.

[163] William A. Barry, "Spiritual Direction and Pastoral Counseling," *Pastoral Psychology* 26 (Fall 1977): 6.

[164] Barry and Connolly, *Spiritual Direction,* p. 46.

[165] Ibid., pp. 63, 41; Dyckman, *Inviting the Mystic,* p. 23.

[166] Dyckman, *Inviting the Mystic,* pp. 43-50.

[167] Isabell, *Spiritual Director,* p. 58.

[168] Studzinski, *Spiritual Direction,* p. 9.

[169] Ibid., p. 9; see also Barry, "Spiritual Direction," p. 7; see also Vanderwall, *Spiritual Direction,* p. 5.

[170] Dyckman, *Inviting the Mystic,* p. 26.

[171] Vanderwall, *Spiritual Direction,* p. 12.

[172] See Martin Buber, *I and Thou* trans. with a prologue by Walter Kaufman (New York: Charles Scribner's Sons, 1970).

[173] Studzinski, *Spiritual Direction,* pp. 56, 74.

[174] Ibid., p. 56.

[175] Gerald O'Collins, *The Second Journey: Spiritual Awareness and the Mid-Life Crisis* (New York: Paulist Press, 1978), pp. 52-53.

[176] Studzinski, *Spiritual Direction,* p. 77.

[177] Laplace, *Spiritual Direction,* p. 56.

[178] James W. Fowler, Stages of Faith: *The Psychology of Human Development and the Quest for Meaning* (San Francisco: Harper & Row, 1981), p. 237.

[179] Hinson, "Spiritual Guide," p. 28; Jones, *Spiritual Direction,* p. 50.

[180] Jones, *Spiritual Direction,* p. 17; Barry and Connolly, *Spiritual Direction,* p. 137; Sudbrack, *Spiritual Guidance,* p. 49.

[181] Kelsey, *Companions,* p. 25.

[182] Studzinski, *Spiritual Direction,* p. 123.

[183] Sudbrack, *Spiritual Guidance,* p. 17; Dyckman, *Inviting the Mystic,* p. 8.

[184] See Dyckman, *Inviting the Mystic,* pp. 23-24; Isabell, *Spiritual Director,* p. 40; Vanderwall, *Spiritual Direction,* p. 69; Hinson, "Spiritual Guide," p. 40

[185] Simon Weil, *Waiting on God,* p.53 as cited in Jones, *Spiritual Direction,* p. 111.)

[186] Studzinski, *Spiritual Direction,* p. 127.

[187] Kelsey, *Companions,* p. 25; Jones, *Spiritual Direction,* p. 87; Sudbrack, *Spiritual Guidance,* p. 13; Vanderwall, *Spiritual Direction,* p.4.

[188] Fairchild, "Spiritual Director," p. 30.

[189] Leech, *Soul Friend,* p.27.

[190] Jones, *Spiritual Direction,* p. 14.

[191] Hinson, 'Spiritual Guide," p. 31.

[192] Studzinski, *Spiritual Direction,* p. 133; Leech, *Soul Friend,* p. 30.

[193] See Studzinski, *Spiritual Direction,* p. 4.

[194] Kelsey, *Companions,* p. 177.)

[195] Fairchild, "Spiritual Director," p. 29.

[196] See Elias, *Psychology and Religion,* p. 36.

[197] Ibid., p. 8; see Robert Yorke O'Brien, *Clarity in Religious* Education (Birmingham: Religious Education Press, 1978), p. 4.

[198] Elias, *Psychology and Religion,* p. 36.

[199] Simmons, "The Quiet Journey," p. 14.

[200] Lewis J. Sherrill, *The Gift of Power* (New York: Macmillan and Co., 1955), p. 62.

[201] Edwards, *Spiritual Friend,* p. 32; Leech, *Soul Friend,* p. 35.

[202] Leon McKenzie, *The Religious Education of Adults* (Birmingham: Religious Education Press, 1982), p. 19.

[203] Kelsey, *Companions*, p. 13.

[204] Ibid., p. ix.

[205] Cully, *Education for Spiritual Growth*, p. 28; see also James Michael Lee, *The Spirituality of the Religious Educator*, p. 19.

[206] Kelsey, *Companions*, p. 14; Parker J. Palmer, *To Know As We Are Known: A Spirituality of Education*, pp. 27, 29.

[207] Kelsey, *Companions*, p. 19.

[208] Ibid.

[209] See Lee, *Religious Educator*, p. 45.

[210] Hinson, 'Spiritual Guide', p. 38.

[211] Cully, *Education for Spiritual Growth*, p. 39.

[212] Palmer, *Education*, p. 10.

[213] Edwards, *Spiritual Friend*, p. 16.

[214] Palmer, *Education*, p. 10.

[215] Paul Tillich, *Theology of Culture*, ed. Robert C. Kimail (New York: Oxford University Press, 1959), p. 6; cf., Lee, *Religious Educator*, p. 32.

[216] McKenzie, *Religious Education*, p. 19; Girzaitis, "Adult Reflective Growth," p. 226, argued that even the use of the term 'religious' in religious education tends to add inflexible boundaries to an experience that needs to address the broader dimensions of the meaning of religious.

[217] See McKenzie, *Religious Education*, pp. 17-18, 20.

[218] O'Brien, *Religious Education*, p. 33.

[219] Grisco, "Religious Education, p. 125; Elias, *Psychology and Religious Education*, p. 7.

[220] Lee, *Religious Educator*, p. 25.

[221] Kelsey, *Companions*, p. 177.

[222] Cf., Robert W. Wingard, "An International Model For Teaching in the Church, *Quarterly Review* 2 (Summer, 1982): 47.

[223] Cf., Girzaitis, "Adult Reflective Growth", pp. 226-227.

[224] See Thomas F, O'Meara, 'Religious Education for Maturity, The Presence of Grace," *Religious Education* 68 (July—August 1973): 462; Grieco, "Religious Education," p. 138.

[225] Kelsey, *Can Christians Be Educated?* compiled and ed. Harold W. Burgess (Birmingham: Religious Education Press, 1977, P. 9.

[226] See H. Richard Niebuhr, *Christ and Culture* (New York: Harper & Brothers, 1951), p. 77 where he alluded that reliance on human reason for salvation is not only inadequate, but even '. . . erroneous and deceptive.'; see Palmer, *Education*, pp. 36-37 for a discussion on the type of education fosters this affective—cognitive dichotomy.

[227] Westerhoff, 'Spiritual Educator,' p. 48.

[228] See McKenzie, *Religious Educator*, p. 17.

[229] See Cully, *Education for Spiritual Growth*, p. 121.

[230] Kelsey, *Can Christians Be Educated*?, p. 29; Cf., McKenzie, *Religious Education*, p. 17.

[231] See John H. Westerhoff III, "Toward a Definition of Christian Education." in *A Colloquy on Christian Education*, ed. John H. Westerhoff III (Philadelphia: A Pilgrim Press *Book*, United Church Press, 1972), p. 60 where he contrasted the classic European educational view of education as an intellectual enterprise with early Hebrew education which was viewed as a means by which a person was aided in growing into the likeness of God.

[232] See John 10:10 in which Jesus' statement implies just such an awareness.

[233] Girzaitis, "Adult Reflective Growth," p. 226.

[234] Simmons, "The Quiet Journey," p. 142.

[235] Cf., O'Meara, "Religious Education," p. 456.

[236] Dyckman, *Inviting the Mystic*, p. 15.

[237] William A. Barry, "Prayer in Pastoral Care: A Contribution From the Tradition of Spiritual Direction," *The Journal of Pastoral Care* 31 (June 1977): 92.

[238] Westerhoff, "Spiritual Educator," p. 50.

[239] In Allport's terminology maturity involves a movement from egoism to altruism, see Allport, *Becoming*, p. 30.

[240] See Philip H. Phenix, "Education of Faith," in A Colloquy on Christian Education, p. 42; Cully, *Education for Spiritual Growth*, p, 99.

[241] Cf., Howard Clinebell, Jr., "Revisioning the Future of Spirit—Centered Pastoral Care and Counseling," in *Spiritual Dimensions of Pastoral Care*, p. 112.

[242] Westerhoff, "Spiritual Educator," p. 47; Simmons, "Human Development," p. 569; Jones, *Spiritual Development*, p. 26; Dyckman, *Inviting the Mystic*, p. 18.

[243] See Whitehead, *Life Patterns*, p. 150; Cf., Laplace, *Spiritual Direction*, p. 100.

[244] See Randolph Crump Miller, *Christian Nurture and the Church* (New York: Charles Scribner & Sons, p. 163.

[245] Charles R. Foster, *Teaching in the Community of Faith* (Nashville: Abingdon Press, 1982), p. 118.

[246] Westerhoff, "Spiritual Educator," p. 51; Cf., Cully, *Education for Spiritual Growth*, p. 27.

[247] The history of spiritual development has attested to the contributions of lay persons in this area, which is the basic premise of the books by Kenneth Leech and Tilden Edwards.

[248] Whitehead, *Life Patterns*, p. 141.

[249] Roy H. Ryan, "Implications of a Theology of the Church for Methodology in Adult Christian Education," *Religious Education* 71 (November-December 1976): 592.

[250] Palmer, *Education*, p. 18; Cf., Poster, *Teaching in the Community of Faith,* p. 111; Cf., Palmer, *Education*, p. 37ff, on how present education does not foster (indeed, opposes) community.

[251] Henri J. M. Nouwen, *Creative Ministry* (Garden City, N.Y.: Doubleday, 1971), p. 4.

[252] Robert W. Wingard, "An Incarnational Model for Teaching in the Church," p. 47.

[253] See Kelsey, *Can Christians Be Educated?*, p. 10.

[254] Hinson, "Spiritual Guide," pp. 26-27.

[255] See Fairchild, "Spiritual Director," p. 29 for a good treatment on this; see also Alastair Campbell, *Rediscovering Pastoral Care* (Philadelphia: Westminster Press, 1981), pp. 41ff.; see also Findley B. Edge, *The Doctrine of the Laity* (Nashville: Convention Press, 1985.

[256] Jones, *Spiritual Direction*, p. 18.

[257] See Studzinski, *Spiritual Direction*, p. 123; Palmer; *Education*, pp. 41-46, 57ff.; Israel Galindo, *Stories of the Desert Fathers: Ancient Wit and Wisdom for Today's Confusing Times* (Atlanta: Educational Consultants, 2015.

[258] For a fuller treatment on the student as content see Paulo Freire, *Education for Critical Consciousness,* trans. M. B. Ramos, L. Bigwood, and M. Marshall (New York: The Seabury Press, 1973); p. 28ff., and Paulo Freire, "Education, Liberation, and the Church," *Religious Education* 79 (Fall 1984): 528.

[259] Kelsey, *Companions*, p. 194.

[260] Girzaitis, "Adult Reflective Growth," p. 337.

[261] Clift, *Jung And Christianity*, p. 81.

[262] Moreno, *Jung, Gods and Modern Man*, p. 36.

[263] Jacobi, *The Psychology of C. G. Jung*, p. 143.

[264] See for example, Morton Kelsey, *Dreams: A way to Listen to God* (New York: Paulist Press, 1978); Morton Kelsey, *God, Dreams and Revelation* (Minneapolis: Augsburg Press, 1974); John Sanford, *Dreams God's Forgotten Language* (Philadelphia: J. B. Lippincott Co., 1968); Louise M. Savary et al.,

Dreams and Spiritual Growth: A Christian Approach to Dreamwork (New York: Paulist Press, 1984.

[265] For a concise summary of Jung's technique of dream analysis, see Jacobi, *The Psychology of C. G. Jung,* p. 80. Jacobi's listing provides a taxonomy which highlights the significance of Jung's technique to both religious education and spiritual direction.

[266] Cully, *Education for Spiritual Growth*, p. 124.

[267] See Clift, *Jung and Christianity,* p. 88.

[268] Ibid., p. 66.

[269] Studzinski, *Spiritual Direction*, p. 2.

[270] Fairchild, "Spiritual Director," p. 32; Henri Nouwen, *The Living Reminder* (New York: Seabury Press, 1977), pp. 24-25.

[271] Fairchild, "Spiritual Director," p. 32; Cf., Wayne E. Oates. "The Power of Spiritual Language in Self—Understanding," in *Spiritual Dimensions of Pastoral* p. 57. Some helpful books on the process of storytelling are: Roy W. Fairchild, *Lifestory Conversations: New Dimensions in a Ministry of Evangelistic Calling* (New York: United Presbyterian Church, 1980); Amos Wilder, *Theopoetic: Theology and the Religious Imagination* (Philadelphia: Fortress Press, 1976): John Shea: *Stories of God* (Chicago: Thomas Moore Press, 1978); *William J. Bausch, Storytelling: Imagination and Faith* (Mystic: Conn.: Twenty-Third Publications, 1984.

[272] Richard Wilhelm, The *I—Ching*, trans. Cary F. Baynes, Bollingen Series XIX, 3rd ed. (Princeton: Princeton University Press, 1967), pp. 224-25.

[273] Edwards, *Spiritual Friend*, p. 174.

[274] Roy H. Ryan, "Implications of a Theology of the Church for Methodology in Adult Christian Education," *Religious Education* 71 (November—December 1976): 593.

[275] Ryan, "Implications of a Theology of the Church or Methodology in Adult Christian Education," p. 592. For a particular method for using dialogical learning in small groups see Israel Galindo, *How To Be The Best Christian Study Group Leader* (Judson Press, 2006).

[276] Kelsey, *Can Christians Be Educated?* p. 37.

[277] Clift, *Jung and Christianity,* p. 128.

[278] Cully, *Education for Spiritual Growth,* p. 100.

[279] Hinson, "Spiritual Guide," p. 38.

[280] Whitehead, *Life Patterns,* p. 144.

[281] Leon McKenzie, "Developmental Spirituality and the Religious Educator," in *Religious Educator*, ed. Lee, p. 44.

[282] Barnhouse, "Spiritual Direction and Psychotherapy," p. 163; Studzinski, Spiritual Direction, p. 70.

[283] Kelsey, Companions, p. 194.

[284] Westerhoff, "Spiritual Educator," p. 46.

[285] Simmons, "Human Development," p. 571.

[286] Howard J. Clinebell Jr., "Revisioning the Future of Spirit-Centered Pastoral Care and Counseling," p. 112.

Bibliography

Allman, Lawrence R. and Jaffe, Dennis T. *Readings in Adult Psychology: Contemporary Perspectives*. 2nd ed. New York: Harper & Row, Publishers, 1982.

Allport, Gordon W. *Becoming*. New Haven: Yale University Press, 1955.

Barnhart, Joe Edward. *The New Birth: A Naturalistic View of Religious Conversion*. Macon, Ga.: Mercer University Press, 1981.

Barry, William A. and Connolly, William J. *The Practice of Spiritual Direction*. N.p.: The Seabury Press, 1982.

Bausch, William J. *Storytelling: Imagination and Faith*. Mystic, Conn.: Twenty—Third Publications, 1984.

Becker, Ernest. *The Denial of Death*. New York: The Free Press, 1973.

Becker, Howard S. "Personal Change in Adult Life." in *Middle Age and Aging*, pp. 148-56. Edited by Bernice L. Neugarten. Chicago: University of Chicago Press, 1968.

Bednarik, Karl. *The Male in Crisis*. New York: Alfred A. Knopf, 1970.

Bergler, E. *The Revolt of the Middle-Aged Man*. New York: Grosset & Dunlap, 1954.

Bilheimer, Robert S. *A Spirituality for the Long Haul: Biblical Risk and Moral Stand*. Philadelphia: Fortress Press, 1984.

Blitchington, P., and Blitchington, E. *Understanding the Male Ego*. Nashville: Thomas Nelson Publishers, 1984.

Bobgan, Martin, and Bobgan, Deidre. *The Psychological Way/The Spiritual Way*. Minneapolis. Mn.: Bethany Fellowship Inc., 1979.

Bonhoeffer, Dietrich. *Prisoner for God*. Translated by R. H Fuller. Edited by E. Bethge. London: S.C.M. Press, 1953.

Bouwsma, William J. "Christian Adulthood," pp. 81-96. In *Adulthood*. Edited by Erik H. Erikson. New York: W. W. Norton, 1978, pp. 81-96. 30

Browning, Don S. *Generative Man: Psychoanalytic Perspectives.* Philadelphia: Westminster Press, 1973.

Buber, Martin. *I and Thou.* Translated with a Prologue by Walter Kaufman. New York: Charles Scribner's Sons, 1970.

Campbell, Alastair. *Rediscovering Pastoral Care.* Philadelphia: The Westminster Press, 1981.

Capps, Donald. *Life Cycle Theory and Pastoral Care*. Philadelphia: Fortress Press, 1933.

Chew, Peter. *The Inner World of the Middle Aged Man.* New York: McMillan Publishing Co. Inc., 1976.

Christensen, Bernhard. *The Inward Pilgrimage: Spiritual Classics from Augustine to Bonhoffer.* Minneapolis: Augsburg Publishing House, 1976.

Clausen, John. "The Life Course of Individuals." In *Aging and Society* vol. 3. The Society of Age Stratification, pp. 457-514. Edited by Riley, W.; Johnson, M.; Foner, A. New York: Russell Sage Foundation, 1972.

Clift, Wallace B. *Jung and Christianity: The Challenge of Reconciliation.* New York: Crossroad, 1982.

Clinebell, Jr. Howard. *Growth Counseling For Mid-years Couples.* Philadelphia: Fortress Press, 1977.

_____ "Revisioning the Future of Spirit-Centered Pastoral Care." *In Spiritual Dimensions of Pastoral Care*, pp. 101-13. Edited by Borchert, G. L., and A. Lester, D. Philadelphia: The Westminster Press, 1985.

Colarusso, Calvin A., and Nemiroff, Robert. *Adult Development: A New Dimension in Psychodynamic Theory and Practice.* New York: Plenum Press, 1987.

Cole, William Graham. *The Restless Quest of Modern Man.* New York: Oxford University Press, 1966.

Conway, James. *Men in Midlife Crisis.* Elgin, Ill.: Cook, 1978.

Cooper, John C. Religion *After Forty.* Philadelphia: A Pilgrim Press Book United Church Press, 1973.

Cully, Iris V. *Education for Spiritual Growth.* San Francisco: Harper & Row, Publishers, 1984.

Darling, Harold W. "Christian Growth: A Developmental Psychological Model." In *Research in Mental Health and Religious Behavior: An Introduction to Research in the Integration of Christianity and the Behavioral Sciences*, pp. 56-66. Edited by Donaldson, Jr. W. J. N.p.: The Psychological Studies Institute, 1976.

Davitz, Joel, and Davitz, Lois. *Making It: 40 and Beyond, Surviving the Mid—Life Crisis*. Minneapolis, Mn.: Winston Press, 1979.

De Sales, Francis. *Introduction to the Devout Life*. Trans. by B. Ward. London: A. R. Mowbray, 1975.

_____. *Introduction to the Devout Life*. Translated by John K. Ryan, Garden City, NY: Image Books, 1955.

Doniger, Simon. *Becoming the Complete Adult*. New York: Association Press, 1962.

Dyckman, Katherine Marie, and Carroll, L. Patrick. *Inviting the Mystic, Supporting the Prophet: An Introduction to Spiritual Direction*. New York: Paulist Press, 1981.

Edge, Findley B. *The Doctrine of the Laity*. Nashville: Convention Press, 1985.

Edwards, Tilden. *Spiritual Friend: Reclaiming the Gift of Spiritual Direction*. New York: Paulist Press, 1980.

Elias, John L. *The Foundations and Practice of Adult Religious Education*. Malabar, El.: Robert E. Krieger Publishing Co., 1982.

_____. *Psychology and Religious Education*. Malabar, Fl: Robert E. Krieger Publishing Co., 1983.

English, John J. *Spiritual Freedom: From An Experience of the Ignatian Exercises to the Art of Spiritual Direction*. Guelph, Ontario: Loyola House, 1979.

Engstom, Ted W. *The Most Important Thing a Man Needs to Know About The Rest of His Life*. Old Tappan, N.J.: Fleming H. Revell Co., 1981.

Erikson, Erik H. *Adulthood*. New York; W. W. Norton & Co.: 1978.

_____. *Childhood and Society*. 2nd edition. New York: W. W. Norton, 1963. .

_____. *Dimensions of a New Identity*. New York: W. W. Norton & Co., Inc., 1974. .

_____. *Ghandi's Truth*. New York: W. W. Norton, 1969.

_____. *Identity and the Life Cycle*. Psychosocial Issues, Vol. I, no. 1. New York: International Universities Press, 1959.

_____. *Identity: Youth and Crisis.* New York: N. W. Norton, 1968.

_____. *Young Man Luther.* New York: W. W. Norton, 1958.

Evans, Donald. *Struggle and Fulfillment: The Inner Dynamics of Religion and Morality.* Philadelphia: Fortress Press, 1979.

Evoy, John J., and Christopher, Van F. *Personality Development in the Christian Life.* New York: Sheed and Ward, 1962.

Fairchild, Roy W. *Lifestory Conversations: New Dimensions in a Ministry of Evangelistic Calling.* New York: United Presbyterian Church, 1980.

Farnsworth, Kirk E. *Whole-Hearted Integration: Harmonizing Psychology and Christianity Through Word and Deed.* Grand Rapids: Baker Book House, 1985.

Finley, James. *Merton's Place of Nowhere: A Search for God Through Awareness of the True Self.* Notre Dame, Ind.: Ave Maria Press, 1978.

Fisher, Kathleen R. *The Inner Rainbow: The Imagination in Christian Life.* New York: Paulist Press, 1983.

Fiske, Marjorie. "Changing Hierarchies of Commitment in Adulthood." In *Themes of Work and Love in Adulthood,* pp. 238-64. Edited by Neil J. Smelser and Erik Erikson. Cambridge, Mass.: Harvard University Press, 1980.

Foster, Charles, R. *Teaching in the Community of Faith.* Nashville: Abington Press, 1982.

Fowler, James w., and Keen, Sam. *Life Maps: Conversations on the Journey of Faith.* Waco, Texas; Word Books, 1978.

Fowler, James W., and Vergote, Antoine. *Toward Moral and Religious Maturity.* Morristown, N.J.: Silver Burdett, 1980.

Fowler, James W. *Becoming Adult, Becoming Christian: Adult Development and Christian Faith.* San Francisco: Harper & Row, 1984.

_____. "Faith and the Structuring of Meaning." In *Toward Moral and Religious Maturity,* pp. 51-85. Edited by Fowler, James W., and Vergote, Antoine. Morristown, N.J.: Silver Burdett, 1980.

_____. *Stages of Faith: The Psychology of Human Development and the Quest for Meaning.* San Francisco; Harper & Row, 1981.

_____. *Trajectories of Faith.* Nashville: Abington Press, 1980.

Freire, Paulo. *Education for Critical Consciousness.* Translated by M. S. Ramos, L. Bigwood, and M. Marshall. New York: The Seabury Press, 1973.

Fried, Barbara. *The Middle-Age Crisis.* New York: Harper & Row, Publishers, 1976.

Fromm, Erich. *The Heart of Man: Its Genius for Good and Evil.* New York: Harper & Row, Publishers, 1964.

Galindo, Israel. *How To Be the Best Study Group Leader.* Valley Forge: Judson Press, 2006.

_____. *Stories of the Desert Fathers: Ancient Wit and Wisdom for Today's Confusing Times.* Atlanta: Educational Consultants, 2015.

Goldman, Ronald. *Readiness for Religion.* New York: Seabury Press, 1965.

Gooden, Winston. "Responses From an Adult Development Perspective." In *Faith Development in the Adult Life Cycle,* pp. 85-119. Edited by Kenneth Stokes. New York; W. H. Sadlier, 1982.

Gould, Roger. *Transformations: Growth and Change in Adult Life.* New York: Simon and Schuster, 1978.

Gratton, Carolyn. *Guidelines for Spiritual Direction.* Volume 3 of *Studies in Formative Spirituality.* Edited by Van Kaam, A., and Muto, S. Denville, N.J.: Dimension Books, 1980.

Groome, Thomas H. *Christian Religious Education.* San Francisco: Harper & Row, 1980.

Gruen, Walter. "Adult Personality: An Empirical Study of Erikson's Theory of Ego Development." In *Personality in Middle and Late Life,* pp. 1-14. Edited by Neugarten, B. L. Berkowitz, H.: Crotty: W.; Gruen, W.; Gutman, D.; Lubin, M.; Miller, D; Peck, R.; Rosen, J.; Stukin, A.; Tobin, S. New York: Prentice-Hall: Atherton Press, 1964.

Hammarskjold Dag. *Markings.* Translated by L. Sjoberg, and W. H: Auden. London: Faber and Faber, 1964.

Hannah, Barbara. *Encounters with the Soul: Active Imagination As Developed By C. C. Jung.* Santa Monica, Ca.: Sigo Press, 1981.

Harned, David Baily. *Images For Self-Recognition: The Christian As Player, Sufferer, and Vandal.* New York: Seabury Press, l977.

Hart, N. Thomas. *The Art of Christian Listening.* New York: Paulist Press, 1980.

Hill, Henry. *Surviving the Male Mid-Life Crisis.* New York: Thomas Y. Crowell, 1977.

Hiltner, Seward. *Self-Understanding Through Psychology and Religion.* New York: Charles Scribner's Sons, 1951.

Hinson, E. Glenn. "Puritan Spirituality." In *Protestant Spiritual Traditions*, pp. 165-82. Edited by P. C, Senn. New York: Paulist Press, 1986.
_____. "Recovering the Pastor's Role as spiritual Guide." In *Spiritual Dimensions of Pastoral Care.* Edited by G. L. Borchert and A. D. Lester. Philadelphia: Westminster Press, 1985.
Hulme, William E. "Pastoral Care as Nurturing Spirituality in an Alien Culture." In *Spiritual Dimensions of Pastoral Care,* pp. 42-55. Edited by G. L. Borchert and A. D. Lester. Philadelphia: Westminster Press, 1985.
Ignatius of Loyola. *The Spiritual Exercises of Ignatius of Loyola.* Translated by A. Mottola with an Introduction by R. W. Gleason. New York: Doubleday & Co.: Image Books, 1964.
_____. *The Spiritual Exercises of St. Ignatius.* Translated by L. J. Puhl. Chicago: Loyola University Press, 1951.
Isabell, Damien. *The Spiritual Director: A Practical Guide.* Chicago: Franciscan Herald Press, 1976.
Ivans, Dan. *Model for Christian Wholeness.* Nashville: Broadman Press, 1985.
Jackson, Gordon E. *Pastoral Care and Process Theology.* Lanham, MD.: University Press of America, Inc., 1981.
Jacobi, Jolande. *The Psychology of C. G. Jung.* Revised ed. New Haven: Yale University Press, 1962.
Jacques, Elliot. "Death and the Mid-Life Crisis." *International Journal of Psychoanalysis* 46 (October l965):502-14. Reprinted in *Death: Interpretations,* pp. 140-65. Edited by Hendrik Ruitenbeek. New York: Dell Publishing Co., 1969.
_____. "The Mid-life Crisis." In *The Course of Life: Psychoanalytic Contributions Toward Understanding Personality Development.* Vol. 3, *Adulthood and The Aging Process,* pp. 1-23. Ed. by Stanley I. Greenspan and George H. Pollock. Washington: U.S. Government Printing Office, 1980.
James, William. *The Varieties of Religious Experience: A Study in Human Nature.* New York: The Modern Library, 1936.
John of the Cross. *The Collected works of John of the Cross.* Translated by Kavanaugh, K.; Rodriguez, O. Washington: l.C.S. Publications, 1973.
Johnson, Paul E. *The Middle Years.* Philadelphia: Fortress Press, 1971.
_____. *Personality and Religion.* Nashville: Abington Press, 1957.

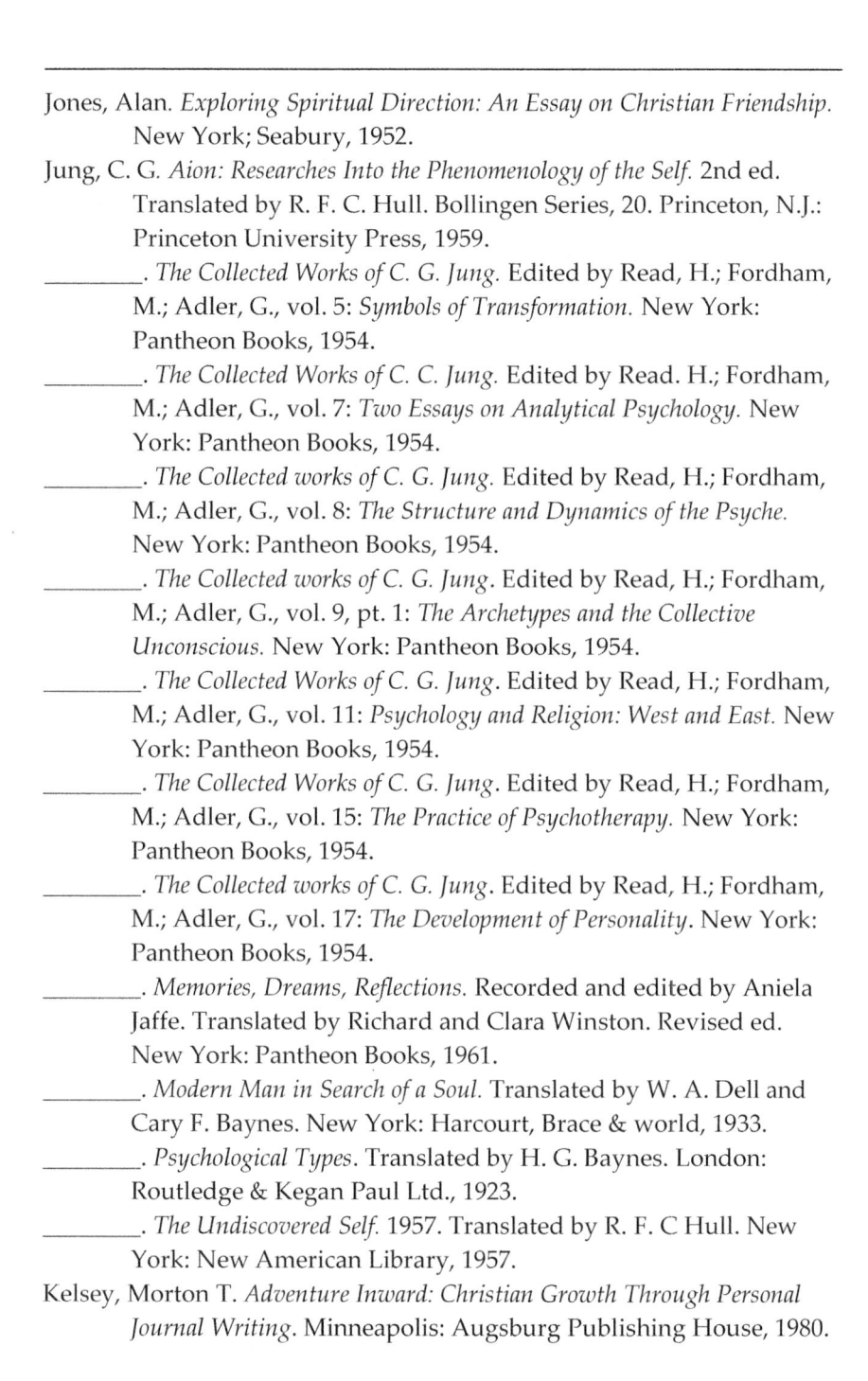

Jones, Alan. *Exploring Spiritual Direction: An Essay on Christian Friendship.* New York; Seabury, 1952.

Jung, C. G. *Aion: Researches Into the Phenomenology of the Self.* 2nd ed. Translated by R. F. C. Hull. Bollingen Series, 20. Princeton, N.J.: Princeton University Press, 1959.

_____. *The Collected Works of C. G. Jung.* Edited by Read, H.; Fordham, M.; Adler, G., vol. 5: *Symbols of Transformation.* New York: Pantheon Books, 1954.

_____. *The Collected Works of C. C. Jung.* Edited by Read. H.; Fordham, M.; Adler, G., vol. 7: *Two Essays on Analytical Psychology.* New York: Pantheon Books, 1954.

_____. *The Collected works of C. G. Jung.* Edited by Read, H.; Fordham, M.; Adler, G., vol. 8: *The Structure and Dynamics of the Psyche.* New York: Pantheon Books, 1954.

_____. *The Collected works of C. G. Jung.* Edited by Read, H.; Fordham, M.; Adler, G., vol. 9, pt. 1: *The Archetypes and the Collective Unconscious.* New York: Pantheon Books, 1954.

_____. *The Collected Works of C. G. Jung.* Edited by Read, H.; Fordham, M.; Adler, G., vol. 11: *Psychology and Religion: West and East.* New York: Pantheon Books, 1954.

_____. *The Collected Works of C. G. Jung.* Edited by Read, H.; Fordham, M.; Adler, G., vol. 15: *The Practice of Psychotherapy.* New York: Pantheon Books, 1954.

_____. *The Collected works of C. G. Jung.* Edited by Read, H.; Fordham, M.; Adler, G., vol. 17: *The Development of Personality.* New York: Pantheon Books, 1954.

_____. *Memories, Dreams, Reflections.* Recorded and edited by Aniela Jaffe. Translated by Richard and Clara Winston. Revised ed. New York: Pantheon Books, 1961.

_____. *Modern Man in Search of a Soul.* Translated by W. A. Dell and Cary F. Baynes. New York: Harcourt, Brace & world, 1933.

_____. *Psychological Types.* Translated by H. G. Baynes. London: Routledge & Kegan Paul Ltd., 1923.

_____. *The Undiscovered Self.* 1957. Translated by R. F. C Hull. New York: New American Library, 1957.

Kelsey, Morton T. *Adventure Inward: Christian Growth Through Personal Journal Writing.* Minneapolis: Augsburg Publishing House, 1980.

_____. *Can Christians Be Educated?* Compiled and edited by H. W. Burgess. Birmingham: Religious Education Press, 1977.

_____. *Companions on the Inner Way: The Art of Spiritual Guidance.* New York: Crossroads, 1983.

_____. *Discernment: A Study in Ecstasy and Evil.* New York: Paulist Press, 1978.

_____. *Dreams: A Way to Listen to God.* New York: Paulist Press, 1978.

_____. *God, Dreams, and Revelation.* Minneapolis: Augsburg Press, 1974.

Kimall, Robert C., ed. *Theology of Culture.* New York: Oxford University Press, 1959.

Knowles, Malcom. *The Modern Practice of Adult Education.* Chicago: Follet/Association Press, 1980.

Knox, John. *Myth and Truth.* Charlottesville: University of Virginia, 1964.

Kort, Wesley A. *Narrative Elements and Religious Meaning.* Philadelphia: Fortress Press, 1975.

Kraft, William F. *Achieving Promises: A Spiritual Guide for the Transition of Life.* Philadelphia: The Westminster Press, 1981.

Kubler—Ross, Elizabeth. *Death: The Final Stage of Growth.* Englewood Cliffs, N. J.: Prentice-Hall Publishers, 1975.

Laplace, Jean. *Preparing for Spiritual Direction.* Translated by John C. Guinness with a Forward by J. C. Futrell. Chicago: Franciscan Herald Press, 1975.

Leclercq, Jean. *The Love of Learning and the Desire for God: A Study of Monastic Culture.* New York: Fordham University Press, 1974.

Lee, James M. *The Spirituality of the Religious Educator.* Birmingham: Religious Education Press, 1985.

Leech, Kenneth. *Soul Friend: The Practice of Christian Spirituality.* Introduction by H. J. M. Nouwen. San Francisco: Harper & Row, Publishers, 1977.

Lefevre, Perry, and Schroeder, W. Widick, eds. *Spiritual Nurture and Congregational Development.* Chicago: Exploration Press of the Chicago Theological seminary, 1984.

Leuba, James H. *The Psychology of Religious Mysticism.* New York: Harcourt, Brace, and Co., 1925.

Levinson, Daniel J. "Toward a Conception of the Adult Life Course." In *Themes of Work and Love in Adulthood,* pp. 265-90. Edited by

Smelser, N. J. and Erikson, Erik H. Cambridge, Mass.: Harvard University Press, 1980.

Levinson, Daniel J.; Darrow, C. N.; Klein, E. B.; Levinson, M. H.; McKee, B. *The Seasons of A Man's Life.* New York: Alfred S. Knopf, 1978.

Little, Sara. *To Set One's Heart: Belief and Teaching in the Church.* Atlanta: John Knox Press, 1983.

Lonergan, Bernard. *Method in Theology.* New York: Herder & Herder, 1972.

Lynch, William, *Images of Faith: An Exploration of the Ironic Imagination.* Notre Dame, Ind.: University of Notra Dame Press, 1973.

Maslow, Abraham H. *Religion, Values, and Peak Experiences.* Columbus, Oh.: Ohio State University Press, 1964.

Maves, Paul B. *The Best Is Yet To Be.* Philadelphia: The Westminster Press, n.d. .

_____. "Religious Development in Adulthood." In *Research on Religious Development,* pp. 777-79. Edited By M. Strommen. New York: Hawthorn Books, 1971.

Mavis, W. Curry. *The Psychology of Christian Experience.* Grand Rapids: Zondervan Publishing House, 1963.

May, Gerald G. *Care of Mind/Care of Spirit: Psychiatric Dimensions of Spiritual Direction.* San Francisco: Harper & Row, 1982.

May, Rollo. *Love and Will.* New York: W. N. Norton, 1969.

Mayer, Nancy. *The Male Mid-Life Crisis.* New York: Viking Press, 1978.

McDonald, Gordon. *Living at High Noon: Reflections on the Drama of Mid-Life.* Old Tappan: Fleming H. Revell Co., 1985.

McGill, Michael E. *The 40- to 60-Year Old Male: A Guide for Men — The Women in Their Lives — To See Them Through the Crisis of the Male Middle Years.* New York: Simon and Schuster, 1980.

McKenzie, Leon. *The Religious Education of Adults.* Birmingham: Religious Education Press, 1982.

_____. "Developmental Spirituality and the Religious Educator." In *The Spirituality of the Religious Educator,* pp. 43-65. Edited by James Michael Lee. Birmingham: Religious Education Press, 1985.

McMorrow, Fred. *Middlescence: The Dangerous Years.* New York: Stramberg Hill Publishing Co. Inc., 1974.

McNamara, William. *Mystical Passion: Spirituality for a Bored Society.* New York: Paulist Press, 1977.

McNeill, John T. *A History of the Cure of Souls.* New York: Harper & Brothers, 1951.

Meissner, W. W. *Group Dynamics in the Religious Life.* Notre Dame, Ind.: University of Notre Dame Press, 1966.

Merton, Thomas. *Contemplative Prayer.* Garden City, New York: Image Books, 1971.

_____. *Spiritual Direction and Meditation.* Collegeville, Minn.: Liturgical Press, 1960.

Miller, Randolph C. *Christian Nurture and the Church.* New York: Charles Scribner's Sons, 1951.

Moran, Gabriel. *Religious Education Development: Images For the Future.* Minneapolis: Winston Press, 1983.

Moreno, Antonio. *Jung, Gods, and Modern Man.* London: University of Notre Dame Press, 1970.

Morley, David C. *Halfway Up the Mountain.* Old Tappan, N.J.; Fleming H. Revell, 1979.

Nagy, Maria H. "The Child's View of Death." *Journal of Genetic Psychology* 73 (1948):3—27. Reprinted in *The Meaning of Death*, pp. 79-98. Edited by H. Feifel. New York; McGraw-Hill, 1959.

Neugarten, Bernice L., ed. *Middle Age and Aging.* Chicago: University of Chicago Press, 1968.

_____. "A Developmental View of Adult Personality." In *Relations of Development and Aging*, pp. 176—208. Edited by James Birren. Springfield, Ill.: Charles C. Thomas, 1964.

_____. "Adult Personality: Toward a Psychology of the Life Cycle." in *Middle Age and Aging*, pp. 137-47. Edited by Bernice L. Neugarten. Chicago: University of Chicago Press, 1968.

_____. "The Awareness of Middle Age." in *Middle Age and Aging*, pp. 93-98. Edited by Bernice L. Neugarten. Chicago: University of Chicago Press, 1968.

Niebuhr, Richard H. *Christ and Culture.* New York: Harper & Brothers, 1951.

Norman, William H., and Scaramella, Thomas J., eds. *Mid- Life: Developmental and Clinical Issues.* New York: Brunner/Mazel, 1980.

Nouwen, Henry J. M. *Creative Ministry.* Garden City, N.Y.: Doubleday, 1971.

_____. *The Living Reminder.* New York: The Seabury Press, 1977.

Oates, Wayne E. "The Power of Spiritual Language in Self—Understanding." In *Spiritual Dimensions of Pastoral Care.* pp. 56-71. Edited by G. L. Borchert and A. D. Lester. Philadelphia: The Westminster Press, 1985.

_____. *The Religious Dimensions of Personality.* New York: Association Press, 1957.

O'Brian, Elmer. *Varieties of Mystic Experience: An Anthology and Interpretation.* New York: Holt, Rinehardt, and Winston, 1964.

O'Brien, Michael J., and Steimer, Raymond J. *Psychological Aspects of Spiritual Development.* Washington: Catholic University of America Press, 1964.

O'Brien, Robert Yorke. *Clarity in Religious Education.* Birmingham: Religious Education Press, 1978.

O'Collins, Gerald. *The Second Journey: Spiritual Awareness and the Mid—Life Crisis.* New York: Paulist Press, 1978.

Oden, Thomas C. *Care of Souls in the Classic Tradition.* Theology and Pastoral Care series. Philadelphia: Fortress Press, 1984.

Otto, Rudolph. *The Idea of the Holy.* Translated by J. W. Harvey. London: Oxford University Press, 1928.

Palmer, Parker J. *To Know as we Are Known: A Spirituality of Education.* San Francisco: Harper & Row, Publishers, 1983.

Peace, Richard. *Pilgrimage: A Workbook on Christian Growth.* Los Angeles: Acton House, 1976.

Peck, M. Scott. *The Road Less Traveled: A New Psychology of Love, Traditional Values, and Spiritual Growth.* New York: Simon and Schuster, 197S.

Robert C. "Psychological Developments in the Second Half of Life." In *Middle Age and Aging,* pp. 88-92. Edited by Bernice L. Neugarten. Chicago: University of Chicago Press, 1968.

Peck, Peers, E. Allison. *Handbook to the Life and Times of St. Teresa and St. John of the Cross.* London: Burns Oates, 1954.

Phenix, Philip H. "Education of Faith." In *A Colloguy on Christian Education,* pp. 40-44. Edited by J. H. Westerhoff III. Philadelphia: A Pilgrim Press Book, United Methodist Press, 1972.

Pratt, James B. *The Religious Consciousness: A Psychological Study.* New York: The Macmillan Co., 1921.

Rathus, Spencer A., and Nevid, Jeffrey S. *Adjustment and Growth: The Challenges of Life.* New York: Holt, Rinehart and Winston, 1980.

Reed, Bruce. *The Dynamics of Religion.* London: Darton, Longman and Tudd, 1978.
Rogers, Carl R. *On Becoming a Person.* Boston: Houghton Mifflin Co., 1961.
Rossi, Alice S., ed. *Gender and the Life Course.* New York: Aldine Publishing Co., 1985.
Russell: Letty M. ed. *Changing Contexts of Our Faith.* Philadelphia: Fortress Press, 1985.
Sanford, John. *Dreams, God's Forgotten Language.* Philadelphia; J. B. Lippincott Co., 1968.
Sauer, Erich. In *The Arena of Faith: A Call to a Consecrated Life.* Grand Rapids: Wm. B. Eerdmans Publishing Company, 1955.
Savary, Louise; Bernie, P. H.; Williams, S. K. *Dreams and Spiritual Growth: A Christian Approach to Dreamwork.* New York: Paulist Press, 1984.
Schlossberg, Nancy K. *Counseling Adults in Transition: Linking Practice with Theory.* New York: Speiger Publishing Co., 1984.
Schneiders, Sandra M. *Spiritual Direction: Reflections on a Contemporary Ministry.* Chicago: National sisters Vocation Conference, 1977. Cited by Roy W. Fairchild, "The Pastor as Spiritual Director." *Quarterly Review* 5 (Summer 198S):27.
Shea, John. *Stories of God.* Chicago: Thomas Moore Press, 1978.
Sheehy, Gail. *Passages.* New York: E. P. Dutton, 1974.
Sherrill. Lewis J. *The Gift of Power.* New York: Macmillan Co, 1955.
Smith, Richard Knox. *49 and Holding.* New York: The Two Continents Publishing Group, Morgan Press, 1975.
Soddy, Ken, and Kidson, Mary. *Men in Middle Life.* Tavistock Publishers, J. B. Lippencott Co., 1967.
Stevenson, Joanne S. *Issues and Crises During Middlescence.* New York: Appleton—Century—Crofts, 1977.
Still, Henry. *Surviving the Male Mid-Life Crisis.* New York: Thomas Y. Crowell Co., 1977.
Stinnette, Charles R. Jr. "Reflection and Transformation: Knowing and Change in Psychotherapy and in Religious Faith." In *The Dialogue Between Theology and Psychology*, pp. 83-110. Essays in Divinity III, Edited by Peter Homans. Chicago: University of Chicago Press, 1968, pp. 83-110.

Studzinski, Raymond. *Spiritual Direction and Midlife Development.* Chicago: Loyola University Press, 1985.
Sudbrack, Josef. *Spiritual Guidance.* Translated by Peter Heinegg. New York: Paulist Press, 1983.
Sullivan, John, ed. *Spiritual Direction.* Carmalite Studies no. 1. Washington, D.C.: Institute of Carmalite Studies, 1980.
Tillich Paul. *Dynamics of Faith.* New York: Harper & Row, 1957.
_____. *Theology of Culture.* Edited by Robert C. Kimall. New York: Oxford University Press, 1959.
Tizard, Leslie J., and Guntrip, Harry J. S. *Middle Age.* Great Neck, L.I., New York: Channel Press, 1960.
Tournier, Paul. *The Meaning of Persons.* New York: Harper & Row, 1957.
_____. *The Seasons of Life.* Translated by John S. Gilmour. Richmond, Virgina: John Knox Press, 1963.
Towns, Elmer L., ed. *A History of Religious Educators.* Grand Rapids: Baker Book House, 1975.
Trueblood, D. Elton. *The Essence of Spiritual Religion.* New York: Harper & Row, Publishers, 1964.
Ungersma, A. J. *The Search for Meaning: A New Approach in Psychotherapy and Pastoral Psychology.* Philadelphia: The Westminster Press, 1961.
Vaillant, George E. *Adaptation to Life.* Boston: Little, Brown, and Company, 1977.
Vanderwall, Francis W. *Spiritual Direction: An Invitation to Abundant Life.* New York: Paulist Press, 1980.
Van Gennep, Arnold. *The Rites of Passage.* Chicago: University of Chicago Press, 1960.
Van Kaam, Adrian. *The Dynamics of Spiritual Self Direction.* Denville, N.J.: Dimension Books, 1976.
_____. *Formative Spirituality.* Volume 1: *Fundamental Formation.* New York: Crossroad, 1983.
_____. *Formative Spirituality.* Volume 3: *Formation of the Human Heart.* New York: Crossroad, 1985.
_____. *In Search of Spiritual Identity.* Denville, N.J.: Dimension Books, 1975.
_____. *On Being Yourself: Reflections on Spirituality and Originality.* Denville, New Jersey: Dimension Books, Inc.: 1972.

_____. *Religion and Personality*. Englewood Cliffs: Prentice-Hall, Inc., 1964.

Waring, Joan. *The Middle Years: A Multidisciplinary View*. New York: A.E.D., 1976.

Weborg, John. "Pietism: 'The Fire of God . . . . . . Which Flames in the Heart of Germany'." In *Protestant Spiritual Traditions*. pp. 183-216. Edited by F. C. Senn. New York: Paulist Press, 1986.

Weil, Simons, *Waiting on God*. Translated by E. Craufurd. London: Fontana-Collins, 1959. As cited in *Spiritual Direction: An Essay in Christian Friendship,* p. 111. A. Jones. New York; The Seabury Press: 1982.

Welsh, John. *Spiritual Pilgrims: Carl Jung and Teresa of Avila*. New York: Paulist Press, 1982.

Westerhoff III, John H. "Toward a Definition of Christian Education." In *A Colloquy on Christian Education*, pp. 50-70. Edited by J. H. Westerhoff III. Philadelphia: A Pilgrim Press Book, United Church Press, 1972.

_____. *Will Our Children Have Faith?* New York: Seabury Press, 1976.

White, Victor. *Soul and Psyche: An Enquiry Into the Relationship of Psychotherapy and Religion*. New York: Harper & Brothers, Publishers, 1960.

Whitehead, Evelyn E., and Whitehead, James D. *Christian Life Patterns: The Psychological Challenges and Religious Invitations of Adult Life*. Garden City, N. Y.: Doubleday and Co., 1979.

Wilder, Amos. *Theopoetic: Theology and the Religious Imagination*. Philadelphia; Fortress Press, 1976.

Wilhelm, Richard. *The I-Ching*. Translated by C. F. Baynes. Bollinger Series XIX. 3rd ed. Princeton: Princeton University Press, 1967.

Wright, Eugene Jr. *Erikson: Identity and Religion*. New York: Seabury Press, 1982.

Journals and Encyclopedias

Barnhouse. Ruth Tiffany. "Spiritual Direction and Psychotherapy." *Journal of Pastoral Care* 33 (1979): 149—63.

Barry, William A. "Prayer in Pastoral Care: A Contribution from the Tradition of Spiritual Direction." *Journal of Pastoral Care* 31 (June 1977): 91-96.

_____. "Spiritual Direction and Pastoral Counseling." *Pastoral Psychology* 26 (Fall 1977): 4—11.

Brousma, William J. "Christian Adulthood." *Daedalus* 105 (Spring 1976): 77-92.

Browning, Don. "Method in Religious Living and Clinical Education." *Journal of Pastoral Care* 29 (September 1975): 157-67.

Conn, Walter E. "Conversion: A Developmental Perspective." *Cross Currents* 32 (1982): 323—28.

Connolly, William J. "Contemporary Spiritual Direction: Scope and Principles. An Introductory Essay." *Studies in the Spirituality of Jesuits* 7 (1975): 95-124.

_____. "Noticing Key Interior Facts in the Early Stage of Spiritual Direction." *Review for Religious* (January 1976): 112—21.

Duke, James T., and Johnson, Barry L. "Spiritual Well-Being and the Consequential Dimensions of Religiosity." *Review of Religious Research* 26 (September 1984): 59-72.

Emiswiler, J. P. "Implications of Developmental Research on Religious Education Methodologies." *Religious Education* 71 (November-December 1976): 522~28.

Erikson, Erik H. 'Reflections on Dr. Borg's Life Cycle." *Daedalus* 105 (Spring 1976): 1-28.

Fairchild, Roy W. "The Pastor as Spiritual Director." *Quarterly Review* 5 (Summer 1985): 25—35.

Fleming, David L. "Model of spiritual Direction." *Review for Religious* 34 (1975): 351-57.

Fowler, James W. "Toward A Developmental Perspective on Faith." *Religious Education* 69 (March—April 1974): 207-18.

Girzaitis, Loretta. "Adult Reflective Growth." *Religious Education* 72 (March—April 1977): 225-29.

Gould, Roger. "The Phases in Adult Life: A Study in Developmental Psychology." *American Journal of Psychiatry* 129 (1972): 33-43.

Jones, Paul W. "The Burned of God: Portrait of a Postliberal Pastor." *Quarterly Review* 5 (Summer 1985): 10-24.

Loder, James E., and Fowler, James W. "Conversations On Fowler's *Stages of Faith* and Loder's *The Transforming Moment*." *Religious Education* 77 (March—April 1982):133—48.

May, Gerald G. "The Psychodynamics of Spirituality: A Follow-Up." *The Journal of Pastoral Care* 31 (June 1977):84—90.

Meissner, W. W. "Notes on the Psychology of Faith." *Journal of Religion and Health* 8 (1969):47-75.

———. "Psychoanalytic Aspects of Religious Experience." *Annual of Psychoanalysis* 6 (1978):103—41.

Neugarten, Bernice L. "Time, Age, and the Life Cycle." *American Journal of Psychiatry* 136 (1979):887—94.

New Catholic Encyclopedia. 1967 ed. S.v., "Direction, Spiritual," by K. A. Wall.

O'Meara, Thomas F. "Religious Education for Maturity: The Presence of Grace." *Religious Education* 68 (July-August 1973):454—64

Peterson, Larry R., and Roy, Anita. "Religiosity, Anxiety, and Meaning and Purpose: Religion's Consequences For Psychological Well-Being." *Review of Religious Research* 27 (September 1985):49—62.

Robbins, Martha. "The Desert-Mountain Experience: The Two Faces of Encounter with God." *The Journal of Pastoral Care* 35 (March 1981):18-35.

Ryan, Roy H. "Implications of a Theology of the Church for Methodology in Adult Christian Education."*Religious Education* 71 (November—December 1976): 583-95.

Schneiders, Sandra. "The Contemporary Ministry of Spiritual Direction." *Chicago Studies* 15 (Spring 1975): 119-135.

Searle, Mark. "The Journey of Conversion" *Worship* 54 (1980): 35-55.

Simmons Henry C. "Human Development: Some Conditions for Adult Faith at Age Thirty." *Religious Education* 71 (November-December 1976): 563-72.

———. "The Quiet Journey: Psychological Development and Religious Growth from Ages Thirty to Sixty." *Religious Education* 71 (March-April 1976):132—42.

Snyder, Ron. "Religious Meaning and the Faith of the Latter Third of Life." *Religious Education* 76 (September-October 1981):534—52.

Stewart, Charles. "Mid-Life Crisis From a Faith Perspective." *Quarterly Review* 2 (Fall 1982): 63-75.

Vaillant, George E., and McArthur, Charles A. "The Natural History of Male Psychological Health. I. The Adult Life Cycle From 18-50." *Seminars in Psychiatry* 4 (1972):382-431.

Westerhoff III, John H. "The Pastor as Spiritual Educator." *Quarterly Review* 5 (Summer 1985):44-53.

Wingard, Robert W. "An Incarnational Model For Teaching in the Church." *Quarterly Review* 2 (Summer 1982): 45-57.

Dissertations

Galindo, Israel. "The Spiritual Development of Adults in Mid-Life and Spiritual Direction: Implications for Adult Religious Education." Ed.D. dissertation, New Orleans Baptist Theological Seminary, 1987.

Grieco, John Donald. "Religious Education and the Male Midlife Experience of Mortality." Ed.D. dissertation, Columbia University Teachers College, 1982.

Mullen, Peter F. "Education for Moral and spiritual Development." Ed.D. dissertation, Graduate School of the University of Massachussetts, 1977.

Rabb, Robert Earle. "A Model for a Local Church Support System for Men Experiencing the Mid-Life Transition." D.Min. project, Drew University, 1981.

Stein, Jan Ohmstede. "A Study of Change During the Midlife Transition in Men and Women with Special Attention to the Intrapsychic Dimensions." Ph.D. Dissertation, Northwestern University, 1931.

Seeking the Holy

Printed in Great Britain
by Amazon